Entrepreneurship: The Path to Prosperity in Business

10 Secrets to Becoming a Successful Entrepreneur

Fitima L. Harris Miller

Entrepreneurship: The Path to Prosperity in Business

10 Secrets to Becoming a Successful Entrepreneur

Fitima L. Harris Miller

Published by:
Millionaire Mindset Publications
2510 Copperleaf Court.| High Point, NC 27265

Editing: Ashley Cannuli
Cover Design: Tammy Luke

Printed in the United States of America
January 2017

ISBN 978-0-692-81848-0

Dedication

I dedicate this book to my loving and supportive husband Warren Keith Miller Jr. and my three amazing children Mariah, Alannah, and Warren Miller III. I want you to know that you are the reason I never gave up. You can have anything you want in life with hard work and a winner's mentality. Never doubt who you are. The sky is the limit for you all.

In memory- To my loving sister Kawanda Rochelle; A true angel of mine. Thank you for believing in me and entrusting in me. I love you very much. Until we meet again ...

Foreword

Fitima gives the equivalent of an MBA to all entrepreneurs while reading this book. She comes from a place of real, true life experience that has provided different outcomes in each. She demonstrates through this book what it truly takes to be successful in business. She is a true testament of struggles, trials one faces when opening a business and the victory one will experience if they are willing to go the distance and have a "never surrender" attitude.

Use this as a guide to starting and growing and building your business. This book provides the answers you seek when times get tough or if you need to be reassured you are going down the right path. It shows that even the greatest have fallen, but it's about how you get back up and never give up that makes the difference.

It's time to get your negative thinking out of your way, eliminate your fears which hold you back, and stop being undecided if business is meant for you or not. You are not your past, so stop letting it hinder your future. It's time to build an empire.

www.fitimamiller.com

Table of Contents

A Brief Introduction ...

I wrote this book to help. Everyone says at some point in the journey of success: I wish someone had told me this sooner. Whether you are starting out your business or are on your way to success, I have been there, and I'm taking the time to tell you what I wish I had been told.

I see two groups of people that will most benefit from this book. If you are just starting out, this book can help you start well and avoid missteps. If you are on your way, this book will help you reset for the next, great phase or it can help you rebound from a setback. One theme of this book is that if you found yourself in a failure of any size or dimension, it is not the end of your journey. You can find success again. This book is for you too. Wherever you are in your journey, this book will help you on your next step.

You will get to know me in these pages, but more importantly, you will see the steps I took. You will learn what I have learned through my own unique, life-long business experience as well as what I discovered through the study of other successful people in business, and how I have applied those experiences in my life. Every chapter covers a key discipline to help you continue, restart, or progress in your business and vision.

My name is Fitima Miller, and I'm here to help you fulfill your vision.

Chapter 1:
Faith + Action = Results

"Every adversity carries a seed of equivalent benefit."
-- Norman Vincent Peele

Hold on and have faith and it will work out. You will get bumps and bruises along the way, but you can do it. In many ways, this book may resemble the counsel of a close friend trying to comfort you after a rough spot in life, but this is business advice. Sometimes we take business very personally even when we strive to be professional and detached. We often take our failures even more personally. Failure or even a rough stretch in business can make us question our faith in ourselves and our vision. It can strike at the foundation of our lives and beliefs. Faith is a huge component of starting a business, maintaining an idea through a tough phase, and bringing that idea to a hard-earned point of success.

I know what you are going through and I'm here to begin by building up and reassuring your faith in yourself and your ideas.

"In business, you must have a deep burning desire for the vision you carry in order for it to carry you through."

I'm Fitima Miller, and like many people, my first and greatest example of faith was in my home while growing up. My father was a police officer. He retired and followed his dream and vision to open a martial arts studio. His gym represented more than just a place or a second career. He believed in the value of what he had to teach and offer to others. He had a deep, burning desire to see that vision through to success and I saw that brightness burning in him the entire time I was growing up.

He taught me about faith. When people didn't show up, he would assure me that someone would. This notion was our bread and butter. Faith was present more than ever when the gym was empty, but he kept working and believing. When times got tough, everyone paid their gym membership last, but my father maintained his faith in his vision and his business. He never forgot his reasons "why," and he continued to strive for success in his business, for that reason. He knew why he started and he kept his goals in sight even through the darkest times.

When I was fourteen, I was running my dad's second business for him. He set me up at a kiosk in the mall. I was hiring and training staff at fourteen. Eventually, what he did with the school and the businesses he entrusted me would prove to be million dollar ideas. They certainly didn't start out making a million dollars, so the faith that saw us through mattered greatly in order to reach that success.

I apply these lessons to my life now in businesses of my own. Faith gets us through the months when nothing seems to be working out. I learned to be strong, to stay still and firm in my efforts, and to rely on my strength as I work toward success. This foundation of belief in myself and my distinct vision served me well at the age of fourteen, building a business with my father, it served me when I joined the military, and it serves me now as I work toward success in my own business ventures. It is of vital importance that we see our faith as a foundation of any business we dare to undertake.

In business, you must have a deep burning desire for the vision you carry for it to carry you, through. That is the only way you can make it through what lies ahead.

✓ Faith is the absence of fear.

Did I just dare to tell you that you are not allowed to be afraid? I suppose I did. This may seem a little bold and presumptuous of me. I don't even know you, right? How can I tell you what you are allowed or not allowed to be fearful of? But I do know you in a way. You are bold and presumptuous. You are daring to go out into the world and create a business of your own. Or maybe you already have, and you are looking to this book for ways to take it to the next level. When you believe in your idea and your potential that much, it does not get much bolder or more presumptuous than that.

Courage is sometimes defined as going forward even while afraid. I do believe, however, that the steps to act on faith are also the steps that set aside fear. Faith and fear cannot coexist, so you are ultimately choosing one or the other. If you are daring to start a business, you must choose faith and leave fear behind. You do not and cannot return to fear without losing faith in the process. Faith is the conscious and deliberate rejection of fear.

"To turn your passion into income is an act of faith."

It is fear and not faith that arouses your doubts and undercuts your efforts. Fear does this at the point that you can least afford it. It attacks your will at the toughest times when you need faith the most. Fear replaces faith when you allow it back in, and they frankly cannot exist together.

To turn your passion into income is an act of faith. It will never be an act achieved in fear. You have to understand that 90% of our fears are not real. They come to nothing. We worry and worry about certain things only to see that they never materialize.

> *"Fear and faith will not stand hand in hand,*
> *so you must choose one or the other.*
> *Choose wisely."*

These things that we repeat in our minds, positive or negative, are an education we give ourselves. We are training our minds. These repetitive thoughts act as drills in an education that we are always conducting upon ourselves. Fear is merely the things that we falsely teach ourselves. Faith is retraining ourselves to believe in ourselves and our individual vision. Fear and faith will not stand hand in hand, so you must choose one or the other. Choose wisely.

✓ Tough times don't last, but tough people do.

Every situation we face seems like it is forever. When we are in the midst of a struggle, it feels like our entire lives. Everything is temporary, but it does not feel that way in the middle of the tough times, especially in business.

You will eventually withstand the storm, and the skies will clear. You will see things out in the end.

At the beginning of any business venture, the path is foggy, and you can't see the other side. At times you will feel like everything is pulling you away from your vision. It may almost feel like you are trying to run with shackles on your feet. You're trying to run toward your goal, but sometimes it's as if you can't even manage another step.

You have to keep pressing on; even though it may feel like you can barely move or even see the path in that lies ahead, you keep going. That is my definition of toughness; that is the factor that will outlast tough situations. Walking through will no doubt be difficult, but you must keep your eye and mind on the prize.

You have to have a thick skin in business. There are times where everyone and everything around you may be trying to discourage you. Even people that should be supporting you may be filling your head with doubts. To make it in business, your belief must be stronger than your detractors. Business will eat you alive if you let it. You can be tougher than your circumstances and you will. You can outlast your trials. The situations are temporary, but you are made to last.

"Somehow someway you will see things through until the end."

It is easy to think you won't make it in business, right up until you do. Going back to fear, we are afraid we will collapse under the pressure of it all. It all makes sense to us looking back at it. It becomes part of our success story. The part of the story we sometimes forget is the most important: how defeat seemed inevitable. The difference between those that make it and those that don't ultimately comes down to who refused to quit. Quitting is the ultimate factor that will make you or break you in business.

✓ Faith is your fuel.

Faith is important in anything you do including business. We often enter business thinking of ourselves as being on the rational side of things. We gather all the data, research, seek out education, and make informed decisions; this is true. We look at our choices as part of the scientific process. We have a hypothesis about how to proceed. We test it and make adjustments in our experiments in the market. However, underneath all that rationale and process is faith. That leap to testing the hypothesis that our business can work is the difference between those that try their ideas and those that dream without ever trying. Faith is the fuel that powers everything we dare to attempt in business.

"You begin to feel that you just might have what it takes to bring your idea to fruition."

Faith is the starting fuel for an idea. You begin to feel that you just might have what it takes to bring your idea to fruition. Faith supplies the desire. You feel a sense that your idea and your ability to articulate it have what is needed to get people to listen. You believe that you can solve a problem that will make a difference in the world. Faith fuels that belief.

Everyone is looking for something. Everyone desires something they can trust and believe in. Your vision fueled by your faith can deliver on that. Faith is the ignition that can get something amazing started. It can be your idea that makes a difference.

PMA (Positive Mental Attitude)

Faith starts with a can-do attitude. My father believed in the power of positive thinking. He lived it and demonstrated it daily through his life and business. He held that attitude even in the toughest times which is when it matters the most. He referred to it as the PMA (Positive Mental Attitude). That has carried me far in life and in business. It has allowed me to use the fuel of faith to get me to where I needed to go.

✓ **Faith comes at a cost**.

Faith comes at a cost. There is always a cost. This is the reason that some do follow through with their dreams in life and many others don't. It is why success stories inspire us so much because so many others are unwilling to pay or even face the reality of that cost of acting on faith.

In business, your faith will be tested, and that is part of the cost. You will be tested like never before. You will be tried and tested in ways you never were when you just dreamed about success but hadn't yet dared to go after it. Those tests are coming, and they will keep coming.

"You will constantly have to decide if you want to stand on the right side or the wrong side."

It is a test to stick by your principles and your moral code. The things that make you who you are and who you are proud to be will be tested. You will have many opportunities to give up those things in exchange for short term gains. Corners can be cut, and beliefs can be compromised. There are easier paths through shortcuts around your morals. One test of your faith will be to do what is right.

You can cheat and step on people to move up. You will constantly have to decide if you want to stand on the right side or the wrong side. Your morals and values brought you to this point, and you have to make a choice to maintain them. You have to fight forces within and outside of yourself to hold onto those things that make you who you are and who you are meant to be.

You'll meet people all around you who straddle the fence. They waver in their morals and trusting them is a gamble for you. These choices and encounters are a test of your faith in yourself and your vision. You have to apply your morals and beliefs every day because defeat will invariably be staring you in the face and attacking your faith all along the way.

✓ Are you ready?

Faith will look you in your face and ask, "Are you really ready to give up all your negative thinking and to become your own cheerleader when no one else will? Are you willing to forgive your past failures? Are you prepared to step back from people that supposedly love and support you, but are really against you?"

"Some people force you to choose
between giving up on your dream or giving up on them.
Anyone that would force you into that kind of choice
isn't worth choosing."

I have encountered all of this in business and life. I have been told I could not do it. My ideas were laughed at. My faith wavered and even felt lost entirely at times. There is no end to the people that will tell you why it won't work. They will always be willing to talk you into quitting. Some people are pure poison to your life personally and professionally. Some of them seem like your best supporters right up until you start to move and make it. They want to pull you back down instead of bettering themselves to rise with you. Some people force you to choose between giving up on your dream or giving up on them. Anyone that would force you into that kind of choice isn't worth choosing. They have to be left behind because they are no good for you or themselves. It is a tough decision to make, but the right choice for your life. Those same people that told you that you couldn't make it will be the ones that come back to ask you how you did it. They will tell other people they knew you back in the day, but will leave out the part about how they discouraged you.

"Failure is often our invisible opponent."

Business owners are the only people I know that metaphorically go cliff diving without a parachute. But that's faith – hoping that the parachute will appear and open before we hit solid ground.

As a business owner, it is a constant struggle and battle each day – day in and day out – to apply our faith when the walls seem to be closing in on us. We have to keep faith when we feel hopeless and think that no one cares.

There are times when defeat stood right in my face and presented all my past failures like a real adversary with an open book of my life. Failure is often our invisible opponent. It tells us that we failed before and there is no point in trying now. Those failures eat at us and try to define us. We can't let them.

"The 'can do' attitude can allow you to see failures as minor setbacks for a greater comeback."

It is at that moment that you have to activate the winner in you. The "can do" attitude can allow you to see failures as minor setbacks for a greater comeback.

✓ **Faith alone will not make you successful**.

I have found that faith alone will not get you where you want to go especially in business. Everyone successful business person seems to have a secret to their success. People think there is this one elusive key that unlocks the door to success. I worked to help people reach success over and over and it was the people who fell by the wayside and never picked themselves back up that all shared a commonality. There seemed to be one thing missing. The ones that lacked action could never seem to turn their faith into results. I began to realize that I needed to teach people to apply action to their faith in order to guide them to real success.

Faith without action looks like this: You are sitting in your living room, waiting for the sky to open up and a bag of money to magically drop on your head to solve all your problems. Faith without action is a plan that never gets started. Faith without action is all hope and dreams without any steps taken to reach those important successes.

"Ideas and visions that sit on a shelf will waste away and die."

I am an action-oriented person. When people see me, I want them to see a "go-getter." I want them to see that I am proactive. I never sit on my butt waiting for anything or anyone to make my success happen. You have to put in the work. I've done the research and sought out the education. It is not enough to simply wish for things. Ideas and visions that sit on a shelf will waste away and die. The passion behind them goes cold from neglect. No one in business will hand you anything. Your successes will be hard earned by all the things you do that no one else may see or notice.

I have reached out to help and mentor more people than I can count. One thing remains true, though: the ones who failed in business did so because they did not possess the will to do the work. Action means putting in the work. Many of us want results, but not everyone is willing to apply the work required. It's now or never when it comes to acting on that burning desire to succeed. The longer you wait, the more that desire will burn itself out. You will use up all the fuel of your faith without ever moving because you never set that faith into motion with meaningful action.

> *"Your action is the bridge that connects your faith and results."*

This means finding the resources, the people, and attaining the knowledge you need to accomplish your goal. Your action is the bridge that connects your faith and results. Without action, your bridge is broken. Your dreams of becoming a business owner will become more and more distant from reality.

✓ You can have results or excuses, but you can't have both.

Just like fear and faith cannot exist together, neither can results and excuses. Excuses cancel out results, and results cancel out excuses. You are making a choice. You will only ever present one or the other. If you have results, why would you waste your time offering excuses instead? If you have excuses, it is because you have no results to share.

I pray every day that I get the outcome I intended for my business. The reality is that sometimes the ballot box does not have your name listed as the next successful business owner in that field.

Hear what I am saying; this is critical. I said successful in that business of that field. We can react to a failure in one of two ways. We can make excuses and thereby excuse ourselves from more work, or we can pick ourselves back up and pursue different results.

I have started several businesses since I was fourteen. Some did not give me the results I intended, but I learned from each failure. The key is that none of these were my last business.

Once, I pursed event planning as a business. I had done the work and had experience under my belt to make it work. I knew what I was doing. I put together the capital and made the investments to have everything ready to pull off these events. I had a client base that was ready to act. The real estate market collapsed and suddenly the money to put on events dried up just as I was ready to begin. The timing was off for me. I did not make a million dollars on that idea that time. I could have rested on these facts and easily turned them into excuses. Instead, I moved on from that idea and pursued another path. I got results because I did not choose to take on excuses from that particular failure. That failure did not become the definition of me or my life.

The unfortunate truth is that many people will never get to see if their idea would have been a pass or fail because they either didn't apply any action or they gave up on their faith. Some let the failure of one attempt be their excuse and their definition.

"Results are simply a measurement and a testament to our willingness to go the distance."

When you achieve your desired outcome, it is something worthy to be praised. Results are simply a measurement and a testament to our willingness to go the distance.

"People take failure personally when they should not."

The primary reason people quit is that they take failure personally. People take failure personally when they should not. Sometimes it wasn't your turn, but that doesn't mean you take a pass on the next turn. Try again. Try something new. Try a new path to the same goal. Keep your vision and remember why you started. Trust that the tough times will not last as long as you can. Change the way you think, so that your failures are not internalized. It will be difficult, but setbacks and failures do not define you. They don't have to. Getting back up and making a comeback do define you. This is the important action that connects your faith to your results.

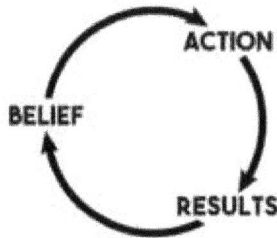

ACTION

BELIEF

RESULTS

Secret Tip: Never, ever forget "why" you started

It is easy to get lost in the weeds with all the day to day that goes on with business. You are always well served to remind yourself why you started and what your vision really is. That is more important than the minor problems you must solve every day. Your vision will keep you energized through all that you must face as you work for success.

Chapter 2:
Taking Risks – How Far Are You Willing to Go?

"Conquer or be conquered."

How far are you willing to go to make it in business? This is not a question of compromising your morals or your vision. On the contrary, I'm really asking you how far are you willing to go to stick by your morals and your vision? How much are you willing to risk to see that vision through? The answers to these questions tell a lot about how likely you are to achieve success and more importantly how likely you are to last long enough to see success in business.

"Leaping and falling feel a lot alike once you leave the safe ground."

You have to visualize the things you want and be willing to take that leap. You have to be willing to leap even when you can't see the landing because you most definitely will not be able to see the landing spot before you jump. You can imagine and visualize that landing, but you will never see the safe landing spot before the leap. It will always feel farther than you thought it was once you are in the air. Leaping and falling feel a lot alike once you leave the safe ground. That is where the risk lies. A fall and a leap can have very different results, and it is scary when you are in the air and can't tell the difference.

Most people don't believe they deserve to be wealthy or have a successful business. Some don't think they have what it takes to have a business at all. You should know that taking a risk starts with visualizing and accepting that you are deserving of happiness. You deserve to land from the great risk of taking a leap. Most people never chance because they cannot handle the feeling of falling that comes before a leap becomes a landing. This is the nature of the risk we must take if we want to make it in business – your business.

✓ Everything in Business is Risk

In business, everything you do is a risk. The difference is whether it is a calculated risk or not. Your first instinct will be to think I am going to tell you that a calculated risk is the best kind in business and that an uncalculated risk is a mistake. I want you to put a pin in that for now because we are going to come back to that. Don't jump to that conclusion just yet. I have a few things to explain to you when it comes to that way of thinking.

"There is a risk in playing it safe in life and letting your vision go."

Deciding whether or not to leave your job to pursue your passion is a significant risk. Deciding not to take a promotion or a new position within your current job is a risk. There is the risk of setting out on your own to follow your vision, but there is also risk in staying where you are. There is a risk in playing it safe in life and letting your vision go. By doing this, you risk letting the music die within you. You risk letting your idea become a regret later in life rather than working to make it a reality now. My father said, "Don't die with the music still in you." Don't let the ideas stay inside as you come to the end of your life. That regret is usually far worse than the risk of failure might have been.

Putting a second mortgage out on your house to fund your idea is a risk when everyone told you "no" due to your credit. This is the moment you have to answer the opening questions of this chapter. Whether you press forward or not is the answer to how far you are willing to go. It is ultimately the difference between success and failure too.

"Faith takes more risks than calculation ever will."

Putting everything you have on the line, will let you know you're serious about chasing your dream. We often say follow our dreams, but in reality, it is a chase that involves hard and desperate effort. Relocating is a risk that involves being willing to chase the dream and run down the vision. Faith allows you to take that risk, building on this principle in business. Faith takes more risks than calculation ever will.

✓ Risk Comes Before Reward

The Real Estate Couple on the TV show *Flip or Flop* used everything in their bank account and borrowed money from a family member to invest in this one house. They did this after they were both out of work following the harsh economic realities of 2008. What a crazy time to risk considering they were already in trouble. Risk never comes at a convenient moment, and you don't get to see the landing before you leap. You visualize the landing; you believe in faith that it is there, and you leap anyway. If their idea of flipping one house that held all their savings would have been a bust, then it would have been Dooms Day for them. They would have been in deeper trouble than they were already in. But if they were right, then success would come. The reward would justify their risk in the end, but the risk came first.

Native Chick Brand was a big risk, and it was my risk. I was going into an industry I knew very little about, dealing with shady people, risking my finances, trusting people would deliver, and gambling with my product. I had to deal with a big-business investment, marketing, travel, and being away from my family and my children. I had to build that brand up from scratch into the success that I'm only just now starting to see and to finally feel the reward from all that risk.

The idea was launched in 2014, but I built up my vision before then. The idea for Native Chick Brand sparked at a time when I was flooded with phone calls from relatives and friends dealing with all sorts of troubles. All the things that got under my skin about the stories of women I knew in my life were translated into tee shirt slogans.

I made the leap and took the risk. I found a graphic designer off Craigslist to start. Three months later, I had my shirts in big malls in my immediate area. These lifestyle and attitude tees I created finally began to catch on.

The slogan "No Side Chicks in the Wives Club" resonated with people in a big way. These were taboo topics at the time. People weren't talking about these things in public, but the slogans connected with customers of the brand. It hit a nerve and that had power.

I began doing some guerilla marketing in Atlanta. I drew some attention and landed radio time as well. After that, we started setting up at trade shows. The entire time I was doing this ground-up building for the brand, I was still in school full time, my sister was in the last stage of her life, and she also needed me full-time.

I then picked up a few rap artists and models. I was working as their manager too and cross promoting with them and my brand. A year later we had a party to celebrate making it that far. I still wasn't done, though. I used every coin I had for the website, the store, and everything else to keep the brand moving. The refund check from my schooling all went into the business.

As of two weeks ago, we had over 100,000 unique interactions with people that liked, shared and discussed the brand. All my hard work had paid off. I had established a real brand identity that I could market and build off of.

There were real and serious sacrifices along the way. All risks in business are not purely financial. On Christmas Eve, my artist had a show, and I was away from my family. The music industry is a treacherous field, and I had to make some choices. I closed down my management work and stuck with the clothing line. The management was a source of income, but I had to give it up for what it was taking from other aspects of my life. I had to focus on my inner vision and use the rest of the time to maintain the other parts of my life.

Native Chick Collection worked because I had a vision, I took a big risk, and I was willing to go as far as I had to go in order to see success. There is a story behind every shirt in the collection. My story and the story behind the slogans connected with people. It gave power to the brand, and that made a difference.

Your story creates emotional connections with people and that markets both you and the brand. Your vision matters in making the large risks you take all worth it in the end.

✓ The Dangers of Overthinking Risk...

Let's go back to that idea we put a pin in earlier. Our first instinct is to think that a calculated risk is better than a non-calculated risk. There is a great danger in overthinking the risk when we try to calculate all the possible variables. That is not to say that you don't plan at all, but there is a problem in overthinking.

"Too much planning and not enough execution can destroy your chances at success."

Don't think so much that you end up hindering your advancement or potential. You want to think of a good plan, and that's great. It is required. However, too much planning and not enough execution can destroy your chances at success. It will keep you from ever starting. You'll end up thinking your way right out of the great plan you made.

You can talk yourself out of anything. If there is great risk involved, it is very easy to talk yourself out of it. You can think yourself into a corner and justify inaction.

One way to overthink is to compare yourself to the success and the story of others. You get to the point where you think "I'll never be that" or "I'm not successful like that person" and you will easily quit – sometimes before you started. Comparison can be very bad in that way. Business will swing you around and wring you out. That doesn't determine your success, though. Other people's stories do not determine your story or your success. I'm disappointed for people when I see them talk themselves into giving up on their vision on these terms.

"Every person that turned a crazy idea into gold did so without overthinking the risk".

Overthinking will never allow you to find and act on that silly idea that ends up making a fortune. Every person that turned a crazy idea into gold did so without overthinking the risk. They went for it instead.

Look at the Snuggy. Are you kidding me? Someone cut holes in a piece of material and found a way to market it into a million dollar brand. Pillow Pets are the same way. Every ad for every crazy idea you see marketed on TV was a crazy idea that a person took a wild risk on and ended up making real money in the end. There is a company called "Doggy Poo." People pay them to go around and collect the dog poo. They did what others weren't willing to do. They would not have ever attempted it if they had calculated the risk.

Calculated vs. Non Calculated Risk

Non-calculated risks are the ones that go against the norms. Calculated risks hedge the bet. Calculated risks typically only go as far as many others have gone and therefore do not tend to accomplish anything great. Calculated risks stick to the norm while non-calculated risks are the ones that go against the norm. The non-calculated risk does the opposite of the masses.

I think individuals that take only calculated risks are the people that usually will not end up in business. Unless they get an experience like landing with Shark Tank gurus that back their risk, they won't go for it. They become wishers and dreamers as opposed to doers.

The only exception in going with the norm in business that could be viable is a franchise. That calculated risk builds off a larger corporation which set the groundwork and the template for the risk. Outside of that, calculated risks are limiting to your vision and therefore detrimental to success.

✓ Original ideas thrive.

Each person has to stand on his or her own. Each idea and vision must be seen through by the risk the individual is willing to take. The original concept sets you apart and puts you in uncharted territory and frees you to create something new.

Where it is preventable, brand new burger joints are not built beside established restaurants. If you try to start your own burger place next to an established corporate brand, they will probably run you into the ground and have fun doing it. For example, many small donut shops don't survive because they do not have the resources to compete with more established corporate chains, such as Dunkin' Donuts.

America thrives on originality. As such, a business idea gets dinged by people in the market for being too much like something which is already established.

You have to take your risks on something original, and you have to be okay with the possibility that you might fail because this is a real possibility. After all the work you put in to succeed, you must be accepting of the end results. The worst that could happen is that you fail and you have to go back to a steady job working for someone else. People do it all the time, and they survive.

You need to ask yourself whether or not you have wanted this for a long time. You have to self-check and see if you are willing to take a risk on your original vision even knowing that you can not know all the variables in advance.

"Business is scary, as it should be."

In business, hard choices will present themselves to you whether you are ready or not. Are you willing to take out the loan as opposed to closing down? This dilemma quickly becomes the moment of decision. It is normal to feel unsure about that. Business is scary, as it should be. If you are following an idea that is original, it should be pioneering. It should take you out into new ground and uncharted territory. Success wouldn't taste so sweet otherwise. I'm not a person that is willing to live with regret, and if you aren't either, then you will take the risk required to find success with your ideas.

✓ Find a mentor.

How do you find a mentor in an original field? If you are going along a new path, who can show you the way? You may be breaking new ground, but you are not changing all the rules of business. Find entrepreneurs that can show you the steps for the basic functions of setting up your own business. Pick someone you won't be in direct competition with and learn from their journey.

You are not copying their story, but you can learn a lot from their steps and missteps before you take your own. Taking an uncalculated risk doesn't mean going into your plan blind or with zero experience with any aspect of business at all.

We all need people who believe in us and support our dangerous leaps. A mentor can serve that role when so many other people in your life may not understand what you are doing or why you are doing it.

Secret Tip: Never be afraid to leave people behind.

The uncalculated risk may mean "cleaning house." Not everyone in your life is capable of coming onboard with your vision. Keeping those people in your life as they discourage you and deliver negative messages to you while you are building something from the ground up is like trying to swim with an anchor.

I would never advise anyone to leave a marriage, but there are toxic people in life, and there are sometimes toxic partners too. If you are being poisoned by these people personally or professionally, there comes a decision point about what to do with a toxic marriage, toxic business partnership, or toxic friends. If they don't have your best interests at heart, you have to decide what is best for you. Sometimes you have to walk away. Sometimes you have to start over.

Today's dreams will become tomorrow's realities. The only permanent thing in life is change. Risk is accepting and adapting to change. Either we conquer our fears of taking that risk or we are conquered by that fear. The place where dreams become tomorrow's reality is on the other side of that fear.

Exhibit A: Risk Analysis

33

Chapter 3:
Getting Out of your Own Way

"You have to be like water."
-- Bruce Lee

When Bruce Lee talked about being like water, he was referring to a fighting style. He meant being difficult to grasp and contain; being fluid and yet incredibly powerful at the same time. He also meant being adaptive and filling all the potential space around us no matter what the shape of things the way water can do with any container. That is good advice for business also.

Adapting in business is the difference between surviving or not. You have to be willing to change your negative thinking and get with the program. The goals that we set yesterday or for next year will change. They have to. The business world changes and evolves far too fast now to go with older models that provided so much more time for companies to change or allowed them to survive without changing at all. We now have to set goals by the month, week, hour and minute.

We have to learn the new technology trends. Don't think what worked in the 1990's will keep your doors open in 2017 or 2018.

Sometimes adapting to survive in business whether you are starting out or you are maintaining a growing business means getting out of your own way.

✓ Getting out of your own way with self-imposed limitations ...

These kinds of restrictions pile up quickly in our lives. When these self-imposed constraints are not dealt with, they will soon hinder your own success in business. They can take a number of different forms.

"Parents do not define your success."

We often feel we are going to be like mom or dad. You may hear that you look or remind people of your mother or father. Some people take this as a compliment while others are put off by it. Your parent's success or lack thereof will not define if you will be successful. Although it is easy to fall into learned patterns, or behaviors that have been modeled for us, their mistakes do not have to be your mistakes. We often fall victim to our circumstances and our family situation can be part of that. Parents do not define your success.

Many people come into business from a personal or family situation of poverty or struggle. This can mean seeing one's parents showing the value of hard work and demonstrating how to rise above circumstances, or it can mean that being shown cycles of poverty which may have made it more difficult to break free to enter business on your own.

I come from a multiracial background, so my upbringing crosses cultures. In the past, it was tougher for me to find role models in business from my community. Opportunities did not always come to African Americans in the same way as other segments of the community, and it was more difficult to make and capitalize on those opportunities. In some cases, successful business men and women had to be pioneers because no one in their families had done it before and no one showed them how to make it.

My mom and sister would laugh at me as did some other family members and friends. My dreams did not make sense to them. They may not have purposely been trying to be negative or discouraging to me, but they had no framework to understand or support what I was trying to do. I was one of the first people on my mother's side to go into business at the age of 14. Some of my cousins still don't believe it is possible.

It is also possible for parents' success to get in the way of your success. You cannot let yourself be defined by your parents' achievements. Their bar of success can get in the way of you beginning on your own or seeking out another path from their vision. If you don't end up doing what your parents envision for you, they might not recognize it as a success. That discouragement can be absorbed as a self-imposed obstacle which can ultimately lead to inaction.

✓ Getting out of your own way with your thinking...

Think differently. It can be as simple and as difficult as that. It may be harder than we realize because we have been trained throughout our lives to passively think like everyone else. We are cheaply rewarded in many ways for accepting the groupthink. Over the course of our lives, we actively participate in conforming our minds to the patterns of thought of everyone else. In the end, participation in the obstacle of "same thinking" is a choice we make. Eventually, it becomes the easier option, and it can be the choice that ends our survival in business.

"Thinking differently will become your greatest asset to achieving the success you desire."

When I was growing up, it was not okay to think differently. We had to think like everyone else. We became afraid to think for ourselves as if it was a bad thing. We are taught to go to school to learn how to get a job. It is rarely taught as an option to break out of that mold and to start your own business. That notion is left in the abstract, and it is viewed as something that is done by outliers. The curriculum in the schools from elementary on up is centered around the idea of learning to work for someone else. Schools are designed around a rote, authoritarian model that prepares everyone to think like a worker under a boss answering to someone else's vision.

Starting a business is out of the norm. You don't even really learn that in most MBA programs. I had to break free of my conditioned thinking in order to start my own business. I enrolled in my program at 32 and graduated at 33. I was not looking to work under someone else after that commitment and effort. That wasn't my vision. When everyone is going one direction, you have to find a way to go another to get different results and to cut a different path.

Thinking differently will become your greatest asset to achieving the success you desire. If I thought like everyone else, I would not be the woman I am today. Out of the box, thinking is imperative to giving you a running start in business. It is essential for moving your vision forward and for building a business in the current rapid evolution of the market.

"People sometimes break patterns,
but never really changed their way of thinking."

You have to control your own mind and thought processes. People sometimes break patterns, but never really changed their way of thinking. Old thinking and same thinking are still in their way even as they try to go in a different direction.

I gained a half million dollar house but eventually lost it after an unfortunate turn in the economy. I always intended to get it back. My state of mind was never one of defeat. Others have the opposite problem. Even when they do strike out on their own and achieve success, they are still stuck in old ways of thinking. When trouble comes, and they face a setback, it feeds into a mindset of defeat which they still carry with them. That person will not pick back up and fight back because they are falling to the level of their thinking.

"You have to believe your own myth."

You must have the mindset that nothing can stop you. You go out believing you are the best and the biggest and that no one out there has the power to keep you down. You can't think of yourself as small while you are on the rise. You have to have a mindset that does not accept defeat long before you ever reach success. You have to believe your own myth.

You have to believe in yourself. Self-doubt and lack of confidence work against everything you might hope to achieve. If you don't believe it, you can't achieve it. The biggest enemy in this regard is the one you allow to live inside your own head. You begin to hear voices that say, "Can't. Don't. No one else in your family has made it. Who would take a chance on you with your history and credit?"

When taking that step to become a business owner, you have no room for self-doubt. You will kill your dream before you ever start. Business is not for the weak or faint. You have to believe that you can go against the biggest fish in business. You have to believe you are just as good, if not better.

Muhammad Ali was one of the greatest boxers of all time. He was famous for showing confidence and removed all self-doubt before a fight. He would scare his opponents through mere conversation. If he wasn't the best, you would have thought he was after all the "smack" he talked to the commentators and other fighters. Eventually, he became the best. There is simply no way he would have achieved so many successful knockouts if he did not believe in himself as he prepared for his fights.

✓ Getting out of your own way with thinking too small ...

Thinking big is not the same thing as thinking differently. You can think differently but still, think way too small. You can have a great idea with the potential to change lives, but still only think on a neighborhood level when you should be thinking on a global level.

> *"Change your thinking; change your mind to change your outcome."*

If you're going to make it in business, you have to think on a global scale. When I started many of my businesses, I never thought to think on a global scale. I just wanted to help the people on my street or possibly just in my local community. It wasn't that I was not smart or did not have the capability to do more. My vision just began with what was in front of me. The problem I tackled was the one around me on the neighborhood level, and I had not yet extrapolated that out to the broader world. I often say, change your thinking; change your mind to change your outcome. This goes directly to the notion of thinking bigger.

If you know better, you will do better. This is a key fact of business and life. When I started to think about the people I could help and the lives I could change, I began to make more strides in business, and it changed everything regarding my outcomes.

> *"If we continue to think small in this current world and business environment, there is a serious question about how long you can stay in business."*

With my event planning business, I had a good idea and a good plan. I had received experience and done the research. I knew what I was capable of doing. I would always put on parties for those that could not afford to, which were mainly individuals around me and in my neighborhood. I drew my vision to plan parties from those immediately around me; I did not at first see the full potential if I extended my vision beyond my local area.

If I extended out, I could change the world. Why was I thinking so small? We can and should extend our influence with world thinking. Without thinking globally, we will three like most people are, and that is why the vast majority of businesses are strictly mom and pop shops. We usually just think of the market in our local community. One million can be extended into ten million if you think and act big enough. If we continue to think small in this current world and business environment, there is a serious question about how long you can stay in business.

It was not until I visited the Biltmore Estate in Asheville, North Carolina that I started to comprehend the fact that I had been thinking too small. My personal goal for my rewards and my businesses was to own makeup houses one day, excluding the one I already lived in and the one my husband and I rented out. I realized at that moment if someone back in the 1800's could own 120 acres of land and an estate that massive, then I was thinking way too small in the present. I realized I should want to own a block or even an entire neighborhood. There is far greater potential for growth and reward if you truly believe that you can affect people on a global scale.

✓ Get out of your own way with your excuses ...

The biggest disease in business is "excuse-itis." Excuses destroy potential. My leg hurts. My back hurts. I'll do it tomorrow. I work too much. My kids are making me tired. The excuses never end, and the real work never gets started.

My dad used to make me recite: Excuses are tools of incompetence that bridge the gap to nothingness.
When I was in my father's martial arts studio, he pushed me to achieve when I was only four-years-old. He did not give me belts

easily, and he pushed me to keep going toward the goal of a black belt when I was six. He wouldn't let me quit. He wouldn't let me give excuses. I finally made black belt at eight.

He had a "Negative Box." Students had to pay a quarter for every negative word they used. If you did not have money, you had to do 20 push-ups instead. Some kids came to class with a roll of quarters already in hand. Even though it seemed harsh at the time, it prepared us for success by eliminating keywords from our vocabulary. These keywords gave rise to excuses and therefore negative results.

These same five negative words are words you cannot use in business and expect success at the same time.

- **Can't**
- **Won't**
- **Quit**
- **Try**
- **Impossible**

None of these lead to positive results or success. "Try" is better than can't, won't, or quit, but there is still a vast difference between putting in an effort without truly expecting those actions to bring about success and the idea of going after something with the mindset that failure is not an option. To try is to just 'go through the motions.' They are two very different approaches and lead to very different results.

You have to replace this thinking with positive affirmations that you can repeat every morning to drive you toward real success:

- **I can do it.**
- **I must do it.**
- **I have to do it.**
- **I don't have any other choice.**
- **I will get the job done. That's it. Period.**
- **Believe and succeed.**

You have to think of business as a theatrical performance, and you are the main act. As long as you are on stage and pushing to perform, someone is watching. That 'someone' may not yet be convinced. They may not be sold on you or your idea yet, but while you are on the stage, you still have the floor. Someone will support you with their attention.

If you give up the good fight, it's a different story. No one cares until you win and they will watch while you are still on stage striving for the win in your performance. If you let yourself give up before the performance is over, they are done with you. This can easily translate to your audience as potential customers and other business owners. You can give your excuses on why you will fail before you start, try when you don't really believe you will win, and then give your excuses after you don't succeed. Once the curtain closes, the audience is gone. Your customer is gone, they will move on, and they will wait for the next great performer on the stage.

You owe it to yourself and your vision to give every bit of yourself. Pour it all in.

✓ Get out of your own way with your attitude …

Everything is impossible until someone does it. Potential is changed by what you believe and then is proven by what you go out and do. Your attitude determines your altitude. People not willing to change their old habits to adapt to new business practices and a new market environment, face an ever-shrinking potential result.

A negative or even an un-dynamic attitude toward your business, your idea, or your vision will sink you. This matters when things get tough. When you are backed into a corner, an attitude of not accepting failure will be what drives you to fight your way out of that corner.

I see people all the time that made a successful launch at some point in the past, but never felt the need to change or grow after that. They start, but never adapt. That is an obstacle of attitude. They take no new classes and will not explore new technologies or innovations. Then, they wonder why no one is coming in the door.

Negative attitude toward change means you will struggle. Your survival will be in question. Your goal for yesterday is not going to be the same as next week. You have to have an attitude of being like water to unlock that power. Water takes the shape of the container that holds it. It fills every potential space and water still holds high power. How we perceive change is crucial.

Secret Tip: When you start to take yourself seriously, everyone else will too.

When you believe you have what it takes, you are far closer to actually having what it takes. You have to believe you are the greatest before you can ever become the greatest. While you are on stage, keep performing; you have the audience's attention. They believe you are serious when you never give up or throw in the towel. This makes a huge difference in how people perceive you. When you take yourself seriously, everyone else will too. Sometimes it begins by simply getting out of your own way.

Chapter 4:
The Power of "No"
The Different Types of "No's" We Face

"If it does not challenge you, it does not change you."

"No" has a great deal of power whether you say it or someone else says it to you. If you face "no" with the right attitude, it can give you power whether it was meant to discourage you or whether it presents new opportunities to explain your vision better, to wait for the right time, or to free yourself from situations that might drag you down or destroy your business. "No" is very powerful. In business and life, we often use it and react to it incorrectly.

✓ The No That Drives You

When others don't believe in your vision, you keep pushing. The first answer you will often get from others when starting your business is "no." They will tell you no they don't believe your idea will work and discourage you in many different ways. People that don't see your vision are seldom in a position to give you a "yes."

"You have to decide if you are going to let them put you out of the race before you ever start."

It's easy to want to quit before you start. Why do you feel that way? My guess is that you talked about your idea with your mom or your dad or maybe a friend. You expected unbridled excitement and encouragement. Maybe the response was much colder than you expected. They are not the people I would recommend you start the initial business conversation with, especially if they have no background in business. It is extremely challenging for them to conceive your vision. They simply don't get it or understand it. They could not see themselves doing it; therefore they cannot bring themselves to see you doing it. It is possible that the idea of you achieving something they couldn't dream of is threatening to them. They would not dare quit their day job to run after their dreams, so they don't want to believe that you could either. It is not an idea their minds want to say yes to. You have to decide if you are going to let them put you out of the race before you ever start. Are you going to give their "no" that level of power over you?

You walked into that conversation so excited to share, but you left looking defeated because you heard that one word "NO!" Your other choice is the choice I made when this happened to me. I let it drive me harder.

I decided to open a nonprofit center to help at-risk youth. I found discouragement from all sides. People who could not see themselves in this type of business told me they could not deal with those kinds of kids. They told me it would take too long to get up and running and that there would be no money for it in this economy. Their "NO" drove me harder toward success in this vision.

"Don't let 'no' get in your way, but don't let it drive you off your vision in anger either."

This is not to say that you run around with a chip on your shoulder, trying to prove everybody in the world wrong on every subject.

That kind of attitude is asking for trouble and will cause trouble for you and everyone else. It will also cloud your judgment which you need when you are fighting against "NO." Let it drive you, but don't let the attitude of proving everybody wrong turn you and your choices reactionary. It's not about them. It is about you and your vision. Don't let "no" get in your way, but don't let it drive you off your vision in anger either.

What happens to most when a naysayer tells us that an idea won't work is that we walk away from the idea instead of just walking away from the person. I say keep going. Don't give up. Telling me no means you just lit a fire underneath me that may take years to put out. I absolutely love when someone tells me I can't do it or that they don't think the idea will work out in my favor. It is on then.

Turn that "no" into a positive "yes." When someone tells me no, I see nothing, but green lights ahead of me. The "no" I fight against is the one that makes me question other's intent. Why are they telling me no? What is their gain in striking down my idea? Do they think they are doing what is best for me? Or is there another reason that has nothing to do with wanting the best for me or my success?

If a person is telling me no because my vision is not right for them, I can respect that. It might be best for both of us, but that does not stop me from pursuing my vision for myself.

"Turn your naysayers into hand shakers."

After the 2008 real estate market crash and the losses we suffered there, I went for training to obtain my licenses in real estate and as an insurance agent. As an insurance agent, I traveled to many strange cities working to get people to increase their life insurance coverage. That resulted in a lot of doors closed in my face. You can internalize that. You can take that negative energy into yourself after enough rejections.

You can also turn your naysayers into hand shakers. In business and our workplaces, we face "no" all the time. Use this as fuel to show them that they are wrong about you. Prove yourself to yourself, and they can see it too. Everyone that counted you out will see that you are still standing.

You can go through thousands of "no's" to get to that one "yes." In the field as an insurance agent, that one "yes" made all the difference. That one "yes" can change your whole life and your outlook. It will rebuild your self-confidence and self-esteem, erasing the impact of all those other "no's." The fight against all those "no's" were worth it to get to the "yes" beyond them.

✓ The Encouraging No, Not Right Now

There is also the "no" that is encouraging. This is the "no" that is sometimes actually "no, not right now." That is a "no" that has to do with timing or circumstances. The groundwork is laid, and it can sometimes be turned into a "yes" later. It is vital that you not give up before that "no" turns into the "yes."

People that told me they didn't need my help in one business reached out to me after I became a success coach to help in that business. I had a more productive and profitable relationship with them than if they had said yes to me the first time. We pitch, we share, and we hear "no." This is an opportunity to adjust the pitch or come back to the discussion later. We would never survive in business if we took "no" for an answer and did not work to turn that into a "yes" later.

When the doors closed in my face during my one thousand "no's" in trying to upsell insurance, some of those turned into "yes's" later. Three months down the road, I would get contacted by those same clients seeking me and my services out. In their new circumstances at a new time, they were ready to buy. Maybe they lost someone, or some other life circumstance convinced them to get more life insurance.

My father had businesses that put me in the face of "NO" more often than not. Back in the 90's and early 2000's, his company relied heavily on telemarketing and cold calling. You can obviously guess who was in charge of making those calls. There were many, many "no's." They seemingly had no interest in gym memberships at the time, but later their kids would be interested in martial arts, or they would be looking to make a change in how they exercised.

I was also a make-up consultant for a while. Like many other jobs I had over the years, I worked on commission. The "yes" was essential to my livelihood. My aunt had a cosmetic line that she still runs today. My father and I were able to franchise her business. When I was trying to sell make-overs, there were a lot of people that wanted to give a quick "no." They didn't want people to touch their face, didn't have the time or whatever other objections they could muster.

"Sometimes people in business love your idea, but it is 'no' for right now."

I needed to know why they said it. I had to dig deep and get up underneath the reason a customer told me "no." Sometimes I could keep them with "may I ask you a question …" I could turn that rejection into a survey to find out what their barrier to the "yes" was. We get stuck in our way of doing things and don't try to turn the "no" into an educational opportunity. We might be able to adjust our pitch slightly to sell the "yes." Sometimes it is as simple as realizing that we failed to explain our idea well enough to the person we are trying to sell. Learning how to deliver the concept on that idea may be the step required to get more "yes's." Through that educational no, you can learn what will help you develop better products and drop products that might be unwanted by the customer.

I have learned that people often say no, because they cannot see how your business or idea will benefit them. People need to know "what's in it for me?" or better known as WIIFM. People throw up smoke screens to keep from saying yes because they don't yet see the benefit. When I first launched my shirt line, nobody got it. I was telling my story through sayings that meant something to me and my circle, but I had yet to sell others on why the sayings had meaning for them. The right marketing strategy explains the idea to them and what is in it for them. If you want to be a master closer, you have to help people understand. They may not flock to your product at first, but you have to deliver the understanding of the product to them in a personal way to get that "yes."

Sometimes people in business love your idea, but it is "no" for right now. This is still the encouraging "no" that leaves the door open for "yes" later. "No" in this case does not mean forever. With my NCC clothing line, I worked to get it into retail stores. I usually received a right now "no" because they did not have room on the shelves at the time, but it became "yes" later. They were ready for me when it became time to switch designs and concepts. My turn came. Yours will too.

"The one thing you can't overcome is 'broke.'"

The one thing you can't overcome is "broke." You can talk people out of a lot of different kinds of "no's," but you can't talk them into having money. That could still be a "yes" later when money is available. I would try to sell potential make-up clients the $600 package. They would say "no, " and I'd try to put together a $300 package. They didn't have the money, and they weren't buying. A week later they would come back and get the $600 package after all. Don't ever stop working for that "yes" even if it is a "yes" later.

The "yes" may feel like it is at the top of a mountain of "no's," but it is still worth the climb and the effort. You have to stay hungry for that success. Don't let it die. Sometimes success in business and in getting that "yes" turns out to be 80% sales and 20% personality. Keep going for it. A "no" right now is not always bad.

✓ The Freeing No You Say to Others

Life and business will present you opportunities that are best for you to say no to. You have to know when it is best to say no. Sometimes other people's morals and values don't align with yours. You may simply not be able to connect on the same ideas or vision. You have to practice saying no to those that can and will delay the elevation to your success. Saying "yes" to such a person is ultimately not good for either one of you.

"Five years in the future, you will appreciate that you said no to certain people and situations now."

No can free you if said at the right time. Family that will not be positive to your business or pull down your progress should not be considered as business partners or business advisors. They are still your family, but you have to say no to going into business with them for everyone's good. The same can be true about certain friends. It may hurt at the time, but it is for the best. Five years in the future, you will appreciate that you said no to certain people and situations now.

"Saying no strategically will make your 'yes' that much more meaningful."

A well placed "no" in the present can save you from headaches in the future. If it does not challenge you, it doesn't change you. You should not say yes to things that don't better you or your life. You need to save your "yes" for the things that will benefit. Saying no strategically will make your "yes" that much more meaningful. You will have the time and resources you need to commit to the things you should be doing for your future.

✓ The No That Saves You When You Say It to Yourself

Telling yourself no is another way that "no" can be freeing. It can save you at certain times. Sometimes, ou have to know when enough is enough. I learned from Daymond John that if you're going to fail, it is more important to fail faster than slower. By that, he means we should not drag out a failure when it is time to cut loose and move on. I compared it to running with a live grenade. You are just waiting for it to explode in your hands instead of throwing it away to save yourself. Sometimes you have to say, "Look, I did my best, but this path is not giving me the results I wanted and a change, of course, is needed." You may have to get out of that particular business and begin a new path to find your success.

"When you hit a standstill with plan A, it is time to consider plans B and C."

When you hit a standstill with plan A, it is time to consider plans B and C. Create something else. Strike a new path. A few years of not making money may mean it is time to reevaluate the plan to see what sort of changes are in order. It may be time to figure out where "no" needs to be used.

As my clothing line began to run into trouble, I had to calculate a change of course. I gave up the management of artists who were also a way of promoting my brand. I moved the products into retail spaces instead of the marketing plan I was using before which had stopped yielding results I desired. I had built a successful brand and I realized I had potential as a success coach teaching others how to establish their brands. I had run a good race with that particular line and that business as I knew it had come to an end.

I want to make the point that there is a distinction between quitting and changing direction. You have to be willing to stick with your vision and not give up during struggle or other people's "no's." If you are on a path that does not yield results or did at one time, but no longer does, you need to look at a course change to find that success again. That is far different from quitting or never starting at all.

Steve Harvey ran several businesses over his rise. He had several different companies including a food truck – very different from the Steve Harvey we know and love today. Many of the companies he started eventually closed. He worked his way up as a comedian and eventually headed successful radio and television shows I still watch and listen to each and every day. Along the way, he also found himself homeless more than once. If he did not know when to say no and when to say yes at the right times, he would have never been able to make those transitions at the right times to find success.

Life can close doors for you sometimes whether you like it or not. You have to pick yourself up and keep going. Life changes are things we have to weather in business. You have to know the market you are in and know when it is time to change over to another game plan.

Secret Tip: Sometimes you have to say "no" to free yourself.

Many of us thank God that we said no to an idea or to linking up with a particular business partner. Sometimes we don't know or understand by telling them no at that very moment, that we saved ourselves from further financial hardship. I believe we can all relate to that.

Chapter 5:
Programming Your Mind for Success

"Before you can master your business, you must first master your mindset."

✓ Success is a state of mind.

Your mind has the potential to output what we want and need. Like a computer, it serves based on its programming and setup. A computer is constructed with a purpose or a set of purposes clearly in mind. It's capacity, memory, and processing are designed within specific parameters to reach a potential and to have the capability to serve the purposes of the user. The motherboard, the kit, and the assembly of the computer follow to achieve that desired output.

"It is time to bring it all together."

If you think of your mind as a computer, we have walked through some of the essentials in previous chapters for the set-up. Establishing and maintaining a business are the key components you will need to set up your program with a specific set of outcomes in mind. With those essentials for success in earlier chapters, now it is time to bring it all together. Like a computer, your mind and your mindset have different components and applications. From here, we can look at the coding that only you can do for your own mind. We will discuss putting in positive thinking so that your personal, mental programming will bring you the outcomes you truly desire.

✓ Repetition is key.

"Repetition is reprogramming for our minds and ultimately our reality."

You have to speak it to believe it. The mind is very tricky; it can bring our words to life. You don't just wish a reality into being, but our thoughts shape our actions and our habits. Our speech and our repeated use of language reprogram our thoughts, feelings, and beliefs. That self-coding sinks in deep and becomes a part of us. Repetition of these thoughts, words, actions, and habits have the net effect of changing who we are, the path we walk, and the energy we use to tackle our challenges in life. It changes our outlook on struggles, setbacks, and even our successes. It changes the meanings of these things for us and how we define life. In the end, this has a powerful impact on reality for us and everyone with whom we come in contact. Repetition is reprogramming for our minds and ultimately our reality.

So, it's time to start telling your mind what you want. In training my mind, I have found that writing my ideas down along with my goals on a vision board reminds me every day of what I want and how bad I want it.

This creates a feedback loop that either adds to the positivity of our minds or the negativity. There is a certain autopilot to our unconscious and subconscious thoughts especially. It reshapes our whole mind in the same way that autocorrect begins to anticipate what we intend to say next. If we are accustomed to saying positive things and speaking a belief in ourselves and our abilities into the world, then our minds will go to that place in response to life. Those words will naturally come to the surface as we face various situations. We will tend to naturally jump to the positive and motivated thoughts and words because of what we have programmed into ourselves. In this way, repetition has amazing power for good or for ill in our lives depending on what we do, say, and think repetitively.

✓ Have the right mindset for success.

This concept is paramount to me personally and to my approach to success and success coaching. Your mindset represents the most powerful tool at your disposal. It is so powerful partly because it is the one tool that is out of the reach of others to break or to take away from you. It is yours and yours alone.

"Your mind is the tool you still have when you lose everything else."

You have to learn how to use your mind to create wealth. That same capacity can also help you gain wealth back after you lose it due to circumstances or even mistakes. Your mind is the tool you still have when you lose everything else. It ultimately can be the only tool you need to produce and reproduce wealth for yourself over a lifetime.

Your mind assists you, grows, and teaches you something from three different avenues. There are those which include use, through challenges and adversities we face in life, education where we train our brains in a classroom, lab, or isolated circumstance for use later, and finally, that which we learn when we are not actively using or training our minds. We can learn things, and our brains can absorb information when we are at rest.

1) Use
2) Education/ Training
3) Rest

We face many challenges and adversities in business. Ideas fail. We learn what not to do next time. That's okay. That's business. That's practical learning in the field of battle that prepares us for the next fight. That is the growth of our minds through active use.

We should always be seeking out education and training. The market is always changing, and technology changes rapidly. If we do not seek out education, we are missing out and falling behind. We are setting ourselves up for failure by not taking advantage of the education that is available for us to prepare our minds for what is coming next.

When we are at a standstill, we see it as wasted time. Sometimes it is. We don't want to remain idle. Sometimes though when the carpet has been pulled out from under us, we are forced to regroup. We don't have a direction to go right away, and we have to regroup to gain our bearings all over again. During that moment of rest when it feels like we are doing nothing, our minds are still processing. That moment of rest can teach us something from within our own minds. We can find ourselves making a discovery, putting the pieces together on a problem that has stumped us for a long time, or growing in ways we never expected. We might realize the meaning behind our mistakes which we did not realize while we were in motion. Rest can give us and our minds the opportunity to learn a lot.

✓ A negative mind will never attract positivity.

In science, negative and positive poles of magnets or particles do attract. We use this as an analogy in life to explain why different people are drawn to each other – opposites attract. The reality of life though is that a mind focused around negativity will never draw positivity from life. Negativity in behavior, attitude, and outlook drives away positive results and does not draw in opportunities.

"If you feel defeated in life, you will be defeated."

Negativity does not draw happiness into your life either. If you feel defeated in life, you will be defeated. If you feel defeated about starting your own business or you don't believe you will be the next great CEO or in Forbes Magazine, then you won't be. Most successful business owners say their success started when they started believing in themselves.

You can end up talking yourself out of your own idea with a mindset toward negativity. When I was negative in my pursuits even for a short period, people did not come into my life when I needed them in order to be successful. A negative mind does not attract opportunity, and even if the opportunities did come in the midst of that negativity, you would be in no place mentally to make the most of those opportunities. You could not properly capitalize on them from a place of negativity. It was when I was positive that the opportunities and the people came and I could make the most of those opportunities.

✓ Control your mind to keep from being controlled.

If you can control your mind, then it will be very difficult for another person to control your thoughts and ideas. If you are able to rise above negative thinking or influence yourself and other people, you are on your way to a more successful and fulfilling life. You will shape your reality instead of being shaped or dissuaded by those around you.

"The thoughts inside your head are all yours."

No one can take the idea out of your head. They can't do it like you even if they try to steal your ideas. I've been in business for a while, and I have seen it for a while. I've lost out on certain ideas. If you were able to do it once, you have to believe you are able to do it again. Even if you lose it all, the ideas that lead to success are within you and you can do it again. No one can take that out of your head, and no one can remove that ability from you. The thoughts inside your head are all yours.

Give yourself more credit. You can control your own mind and your own outcomes if you can control what you take in. You can dismiss things from your thoughts and thought processes that do not lead to the positive outlook you need for success. You can dismiss circumstances and people that try to bring negativity into your life. You can walk to the beat of your own drum without others having the power to influence your rhythm or your song. You can walk your own path by believing that you can.

✓ Change your environment.

The mind works differently based on your environment. If you are surrounded by negative thinking, broken thinking, or selfish people, that will poison your mind. It is almost impossible to build a phenomenal business in a negative environment. Remember that negativity only breeds more negativity.

"You can and should pull yourself out of environments that don't foster positive thinking."

You can and should pull yourself out of environments that don't foster positive thinking. It is almost impossible to elevate around people that operate within an environment of perpetual negativity.

"Greatness is not found stuck in these negative environments.
Greatness is found in breaking out of them."

It can be lonely at the top sometimes. That's partly because people that would drag you down have to fall by the wayside. They are not elevating or growing and they never will. Allowing yourself to remain around them in their environment while you are trying to achieve something is like drinking poison every day. You are poisoning your mind with their negativity.

Greatness is not found stuck in these negative environments. Greatness is found in breaking out of them. You have to find a new way of living away from the disempowering nature of these environments and circumstances that will drag you down personally and professionally.

✓ Your mind is very powerful.

You can grant power to yourself. Your mind can make you function as if you are a living legend without being one just yet. There is power in the emulation.

I have a fascination with the history and details of the Titanic. I have studied it for a long time. In so doing, I ran across an interesting custom that spanned the culture apart from the ship itself but did, in fact, occur there too.

Poor people in that time period often had one elaborate outfit. Some of them would put on their fine clothes and all the jewels they had, and they would go to be around and emulate wealthy, successful people. They would listen to them and take in all they could from that experience in a social situation where presumably they did not belong. People didn't know the emulators didn't have actual money or social standing. The poor would listen to the stories of the wealthy for a night and learned to imitate aspects of their manner.

"Become the behavior."

This form of training for the mind has great power in the pursuit of success. You can become the behavior. There is power when we practice acting like successful people. We want to surround ourselves with people we aspire to be like. We go and do what they do. We can see how they interact. We can listen to how they talk and observe how they close deals. Your brain begins to process this as reality; therefore you are transforming as you are watching and doing.

It is essential to understand that you don't simply copy or imitate others in a rote or mindless way; you emulate. This pattern of behavior is taken and incorporated into yourself. It is not a simple copy, but rather becomes integrated as part of your skillset and mental outlook.

People will decide they want to do a deal with you when they see successful tendencies and behaviors in you. You are essentially giving yourself permission to be successful. Your new behaviors remove obstacles to your success. You are living and breathing success at that point, and it becomes as natural to you as breathing.

"What you think, you will become."

If you tell yourself you're going to be successful and all your dreams are possible, then you become more aligned with your ultimate goals. What you think, you will become. You start behaving as if success is already greeting you at the front door. What you think upon, will grow within you.

Joel Osteen often tells the story of his mother's battle with cancer with tears in his eyes. She fought cancer with her mind. Her method was to think what she desired to become. It involved putting Post-its up around her house with positive affirmations. Her entire house became a flowing vision board that she moved through all day every day. She saw these positive quotes constantly, she focused on her health, and she is cancer free today.

We can apply this to business. The more you focus on having an abundance of wealth, success, and resources, the better your results will be. You will be in a better position to start and to maintain your business. This is the type of mindset you will need to start achieving your goals.

My father told a story about a garden. He said for me to imagine that I plowed and prepared the land. On one side, we plant corn, carrots, other vegetables, fruits, and flowering plants. On the other side, we plant poison ivy, hemlock, and nightshade. If I water both sides, which side will grow? My answer was both, and he said I was correct.

The mind does not perceive the difference. If we nurture the positive, the negative or some combination of both, that is what will grow regardless of what might be best for us. In my split garden, some of the poisonous plants are likely to creep over into my healthy foods and cause me real problems. I can't feed both and expect only good things to grow.

It is imperative that we train our minds only to process positive things so that we aren't dealing with half a poisoned garden. We have to be trained to know right from wrong as children. That thought process does not deviate much as we get older. If we are taught something to be true in the past, it is difficult to accept a new reality. It's not until we are taught to reprogram our mind for success that we start thinking in that new form.

"We must deposit exactly what we wish to draw interest off of later."

If I go to the teller at the bank with a big bag of salt and assuming they don't throw me out for being insane, then that is what I deposit. If I come back to withdraw my deposit, I should expect to get the salt I put in plus a little more salt as interest. If I ask, where is my money, I should not be surprised by the teller's confusion. I did not deposit money. I deposited salt. I drew interest off what I deposited. We don't want salt from the bank. The bank does not deal in salt. If we want interest on money, then money is what we must deposit. In the same way, it is insane to deposit negativity in our minds and then to expect to withdraw positivity and success. We must deposit exactly what we wish to draw interest off of later.

Secret Tip: The subconscious mind has great power and can be easily influenced.

The last thing you watch or do at night will internalize and manifest in your subconscious while you sleep. Bad dreams and headaches can come from some of the negative noise and images we subject ourselves to right before we sleep. Read books on success and seek out positive images to end your day. Think of success at bedtime and wake up energized to start your day and grow your business.

Chapter 6:
Learning to Reset

"It is not wrong to go back to that which you have forgotten."

I know what you may be thinking. I followed your advice. I applied faith and action. I got out of my own way, and I even changed my mindset, but my business is still not where it should be in my plan for success. Maybe for some of you things are working out, and you're well on your way to creating jobs for others and building your family legacy as we speak. I am elated and proud of you. Many of you will be like me and success will not come the first time around. And you're absolutely right. You did do exactly what you were supposed to do, but success is not guaranteed to anyone that simply decides to become an entrepreneur. It is already hard creating success; it is ten times harder to maintain it.

"Everyone needs a reset sometimes in order to succeed in business or in order to continue to succeed."

This chapter is essentially for two different people. Resets are important for people who have fallen short in a particular path. Your business is not making money and not where you want it to be. The other audience is businesses that have done well. Everyone needs a reset sometimes in order to succeed in business or in order to continue to succeed. If we are successful and your business plateaus, it is tempting to continue with what you have always done. If you don't reset, you will not do what needs to be done to move forward. This chapter is vital for both audiences. We all need to reset.

✓ Time, Energy, and Money ...

You might even be thinking so-and-so never had faith and I have never seen them work hard as I do. You may think others are lucky and you are not. Many times in building my business I felt the same way.

These feelings are natural. You have placed time, energy, and money into your business. If things start to flounder or the pieces do not come together as you expected or as you need them to, you are reluctant to do a reset. The problem is that you will continue to put in more time, energy, and money without the benefit of adjusting the path to make those important investments pay off. A good reset can make those things work for you again. Our fear of losing our investment will keep us going even in our moments of burnout, even if we are on the wrong path.

"It may just be a step back to look at the big picture."

Sometimes the beginning of our path will go off without a hitch. You reach a point where you have to set new goals to keep moving forward. You don't have to jump off of your business plan entirely. It may just be a step back to look at the big picture once more. Sometimes a change of logo or a name change for the business is all that is required for you to reach that next level. You might need to reset or expand your audience. You can and should go through the business plan again.

People will pull you in different directions from within and outside your business. Your energy, time, and money can end up flowing along tangents you did not intend or did not mean to go. You have to reset to return to positive and maximized results.

Even under a working business, you can reset to find new ways to build on the positives to keep your business progressing. Expansion may be the answer or simplicity may be the key. Seeing the big picture again will help you get clarity on your path. You will understand better what you need to do to be making the money you should be making.

✓ Feel, Felt, and Found …

Let me introduce you to the "Feel, Felt, and Found" philosophy or the 3 F's that I learned working side by side with my father in business. "I know how you feel, other people have felt that way, but what I found out that you're one decision away from changing your entire destiny."

- Feel
- Felt
- Found

This comes from the idea of closing people and deals. You come in with your objectives. I have used this successfully with many sales positions throughout my career and business ventures.

It goes from feel to felt to found. "I know how you feel. Others have felt that way. What I have found though is this."

You can reprogram as you talk. This can mean reprogramming someone's thinking to close a deal or to deal with fear. You can also reprogram your own thinking to overcome your fears and reset your path.

"I know you feel afraid to make this decision. Many others in business feel that way too. I have found though that we eventually reach a point where we have to take a risk or make a leap of faith."

To stay in the game of business, you have to have a kick-ass attitude as Mr. Trump would say and know when it's time to go back to the drawing board to reassess your business. 98% of small businesses are run by a single individual owner. It may seem like a lot at the moment to retrace your steps; many of us don't want to. We just want our idea to work, and that's that. Often in business, you have to find and try a new angle to get a new result. If customers are not buying what you are supplying, this would be a great reason to go back and review your game plan.

✓ Vision, SWOT, and the Numbers ...

Take this opportunity to review your marketing plan, business plans, financial goals, mission of the business, and core values. Often in business, we find out that we are going against all the things we wrote down in our business plan. Get back on course.

"Each aspect should be aligned with that original vision even when you are resetting."

Sometimes you have to go all the way back to your original vision and you should. Look at your vision board and see if your business plan is in line with your original, core reason for starting the business in the first place. Each aspect should be aligned with that original vision even when you are resetting.

You have to do your SWOT analysis.

Strengths

Weaknesses

Opportunity

Threats

The analysis allows you to go back to the drawing board and see what is good about your business. What strengths can you build upon? Where are the weaknesses that need to be addressed? What opportunities can we take at the point of this reset? Which are the best ones to go after for the best results? What are the threats in the current market? This all comes together to let you know where the industry is going and how you can use that for your business. The timing may be a problem, and one threat may be entering the market at the wrong time. You need to be aware of your competition and what opportunities and threats they represent in relation to your own strengths and weaknesses.

"You have to understand your vision, your SWOT analysis, and the truth behind the numbers in order to really understand your platform."

This vision and analysis go hand in hand with the numbers. They all work together to give you a complete and truthful picture of your situation as you reset. You might learn that you need to focus on direct sales vs. the online route. The opposite could be true in your case. Advertising may be required in a particular venue instead of door to door contacts. You have to understand your vision, your SWOT analysis, and the truth behind the numbers in order to really understand your platform.

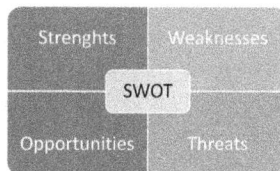

Exhibit B: SWOT Analysis

✓ 3000 Cheeseburgers, 1001 Lightbulbs, and 600 Business Plans ...

I did a project in one of my statistics classes to figure out all the ways to make a cheeseburger with six elements. At first, I thought it would be only a couple variations, but then I opened a spreadsheet. There were so many ways to recombine this simple idea even with only a few choices. That does not even get into what temperature you cook it or what type of meat you use which would expand the options exponentially. That one cheeseburger that we consume can be created 3,000 different ways. Think about how many business combinations you would have to work out and through to find the one that works.

With thousands of options on that one product, you have to think that there might be 600 business options you might have to consider before you decide the plan that is best for you and your business going forward. A conscious reset can allow you to eliminate options that don't work for you and then focus in on deciding between the better fits.

Thomas Edison had to create 1001 lightbulbs before he reached the attempt that worked. 1000 would have been a nice even, round number for quitting. Edison was certainly not afraid of the reset though. You have to ask yourself are you willing to go the distance? Are you willing to reset in order to continue making meaningful progress?

In business this is the hardest for most entrepreneurs to conceive and believe. When you are going through trying to figure out what works, it can be scary. You have to restart, but this time you have lost money or feel defeated. But please believe me when I tell you this: It will be okay.

So you had to take a different course of action. Actually, I commend those who have taken the time to step back to reassess their business. Most business owners don't know when or how to do this key step and ultimately their doors begin to close for good.

The restart step in business allows for multiple things to take place. Review your leadership and management style. Did you hire more people than you needed or you didn't hire enough to keep up with the demand of the workload? Review company goals and check that you are doing work to stay aligned with them.

> *"Sometimes simplicity and a clear purpose*
> *go a long way to achieving excellence in what you do."*

Less is more – are you provided too many services and options to your clients? Sometimes a few select choices will go a lot further in closing sales for you. Complexity does not always bring results in business. Sometimes simplicity and a clear purpose go a long way to achieving excellence in what you do.

This is an educational process by far. Unfortunately, it is not fun at all while going through it, but the reward for doing this will save you money. I want you to think of it like football. You are getting your butt kicked on the field by your competition. You blow the whistle on yourself; pull you and your team over to the sideline to go over the key plays that will ultimately win the game.

You can come back stronger than ever in business. You have thought of new marketing strategies to get and maintain customers, you have learned new technology trends to get your company message out there. Some are quite simple and easy to employ. You may have even learned to go to www.surveymonkey.com to see if you can get real, honest reviews on your products. You can list up to 10 questions for free.

You may find that it's time to rebrand yourself. Maybe people were not getting the logo you created or the name of your business. Sometimes it's as simple as a logo change or a name change for your business. With my Native Chick Collection t-shirt line, I had to consider whether I was confusing people into thinking I was selling Native American products instead of a hip hop line. Proper data and a good reset are important to knowing the right move for your future.

Secret Tip: Don't let emotions run your business.

Building a business starts with passion, emotion, ambition, and a desire to create something special. Once you start running down that path of business, the danger of letting emotions rule you in your decision making process will inhibit many entrepreneurs from creating wealth and achieving true financial freedom.

Chapter 7:
Failure Happens

"Failure is not Your Character."

Let's recap a little bit from our last chapter. We had to reset and see what that meant moving forward. The resetting phase provided the exact answers you were looking for and you are ready to take off with angel wings. Many of you though are truly stuck at a crossroads and looking to shut down your business as the last alternative because that seems to be the best option right now. You're thinking of jumping out of the business before you lose out on any more of your time and investment. Then, you might even think to go get a job and forget the whole entrepreneur thing altogether. I am here to tell you I have seen it all and heard it all. Many of those same ideas and emotions flowed through my mind once. I had to keep reminding myself that: In business, failure can and will happen to us all. We win some and lose some.

"This type of event or change in your business has no effect on whether you are a good person or not."

I want to be the first to tell you I had many failures and took a lot of losses as well. At one point, I spent hours talking with myself that if I had tried X, Y, or Z, then my business would have worked out. Failure happens to everyone. This type of event or change in your business has no effect on whether you are a good person or not, or if you did everything right.

I spent countless hours thinking it over and cried a lot of tears when I had to close the doors to two of my businesses. I did one thing differently though. I soaked it up and went right back out there. I tried something else. I never let failure control me or tell me I would not ever be successful at something else.

✓ Why People Succeed vs. Fail ...

Let's talk about why people succeed versus fail in business. In the next section, we will discuss ten traits that contribute to failure in business. The more of these you add onto your business, the more likely failure becomes. It is a weight that drags down all the good things you are doing to try to achieve success. After going through many of these, I am most certain you will find one or more that you can relate to. Once you find it, highlight it. Then, go do something about it. It's survival of the fittest in business. Let's go to work.

"It does us no good to focus on the things we have no power over."

There are a lot of things that are out of your control. Businesses fail for reasons that are beyond your power. Looking back, you can see there might have been nothing you could do to anticipate the coming disaster or to have reasonably avoided it. Sometimes that is true.

It does us no good to focus on the things we have no power over. People who have an internal focus of control see the things that are within their power. They choose to take control wherever they can and focus on those things. People with an external focus of control see what happens to them as coming from forces outside of themselves. It is beyond their control. These are the people that constantly end up in trouble throughout their lives because every bad thing that befalls them is something unfair that they cannot fix. The system is always rigged against them in their eyes. While it is true that some things are beyond our power, it is not true that all things are. We must deal with and take on that percentage of things we can control to give us the edge with all the things in life and business that we cannot control. In a way, you deal with those out of control things by handling all the things you do have power over.

✓ Ten Key Traits That Most Often Lead to Failure …

Get off these paths. As I said above, the more of these you pile onto and in the way of your business plan, the more likely failure becomes. These are the courses you can change and thereby give yourself the greatest possible chance at success.

1. **Jack of all trades** - Trying to be a jack of all trades … You have to focus all your efforts on one definite trade or skillset. Trying to do everything will mean doing everything badly or less than excellent. Most of your results will come from 20% of your efforts. It is best to hone in on those specific modes of success than to pour your efforts into those other things that represent the 80% that will use up your energy, time, and money without yielding a worthwhile return. In the next chapter we will talk a bit about how diversification can be used properly. Trying to do everything at once is not the way to do it.

This was the one that got me so often in business. I wanted to do a little bit of everything. My attention drifted between multiple, unrelated ideas. Falling into this failure trap can also lead to problems with some of the other traps including self-discipline or persistence. When we get down to those, we will also talk about the problem with following a trend for money and forgetting about your passion which can contribute to ending up on these paths.

2. **Zero Tolerance**- If you are a person with a closed mind on anything, you are setting yourself up for failure. When you become intolerable, this means you have stopped acquiring knowledge that you need in order to grow.

This is not to say you run after every crazy idea or that you automatically follow every piece of advice. If you don't hear anything that is said or you are not open to any feedback direct from others or indirect from data in the market, you will be more likely to fail. You have to use discernment and judgement without being completely closed off to the facts on the ground or other signs that indicate the need for a course change or a new platform for future progress.

This is different from tolerating the unacceptable. Still remain steadfast to your principles and vision. Still demand excellence from yourself and those that work with you. Sometimes excellence means being open to the idea that your current path needs to be changed or improved in some way.

3. **Deliberate dishonesty**- There is absolutely no reason to be dishonest. Sometimes you may not know all the facts, but if you are a person that is cheating people and telling them lies on purpose to gain success, eventually this will catch up with you and your reputation will suffer.

We keep proprietary information. Other business details may need to be kept close to chest. Other forms of secrecy though may be a cover for dishonest practices which cannot be maintained in the long term. If you are hiding things from partners or investors, that may be a form of dishonesty which can bring down a business. Some secrets are used to cover up illegal, questionable, or unethical practices. If you are asking others to cover for you in these things as well, you are not only asking for trouble in the future, you are hurting people. If you have to lie to earn someone's trust or to acquire their money, you have a problem with yourself and your business. If "the truth coming out" can potentially ruin you, your business, or those connected to you, then it is time to rethink everything you are about in business.

People can tell lies about you and hurt you, but that can be weathered. Those are the things that are outside your control, but you can face those things and overcome them with the truth. If the truth hurts you, then that is a failure of your own making. That is a situation you don't want to be in and it is a path to ultimate failure you can avoid through your own commitment to honesty.

4. **Overcautious**- If you are a person that will take no chances and play it safe all the time, you are stunting your potential success. It is fine to risk failure. That is the nature of business. Life is filled with the element of chance and risk. If you never risk success, then you are increasing the sure outcome of failure.

Business is risk. Life is risk. You don't have to chase after every crazy idea, but if you constantly calculate the risk and never act, failure is very likely. You have to take the risk to act on opportunities in order to grow your business. No risk of failure is a sure outcome of failure.

5. **Something for nothing mentality**- You may believe you can put in 4 hours of work a week in your business and still maintain. That is far from likely. There is a reason people that put in more get more. People that are only willing to put in 4 hours a week are likely to get that level of return on their business – next to nothing.

Hard work is required. Sacrifice is required. Those things are within your control. You still want to work smart so that all that hard work matters, but you still need to be prepared to work hard. You have to be willing to work harder than anyone that works with you. No one should be willing to give more to your vision than you do. You need to be ready and willing to work harder than your competition.

6. **Procrastination-** This is known as one of the leading causes of failure. I'll do it tomorrow or later.

We all get tired. We all get weak. We all fall short. We have to get back up. We have to find that reason to keep fighting and working. We have to create our own motivation and drive. You need rest and you need to recharge, but you have to wake up from that rest ready to hit the ground running. You have to convince yourself that today matters and tomorrow is not guaranteed. Now is in my power, but an hour from now may not be. Everything you do for your business on the frontend has the potential to pay off later. Everything you put off has the potential to be a drag on your future success.

This brings us back to something I touched on under "Jack of all trades." We are tempted to run after a trend that appears to be making money even when we care nothing about it. To some degree, it is smart to follow the money. It is not smart to chase a trend that might already be on its way out by the time we get on it. If we leave behind our passion to chase money, we are more likely to procrastinate. This also applies to lack of persistence, lack of self-discipline, and lack of ambition. All of these things can be related to failing to follow our passion. It is easier to get to work and to get started when we care deeply about what we are doing. It is not guaranteed though. Even when we are passionate, there are hard days where we have to find the will to grind out what needs to be done that day. If you find the thing that you would be willing to do for free because it is your passion, it is much easier to fight through those times when things are not working out.

7. **Lack of Persistence-** Some of us can start something great, but never see it through or are what I call "poor finishers."

It is natural for us to get excited about something in the beginning and for that excitement to wane as the work gets hard and you have to deal with the business side of your dream that may not be nearly as fun though it is required. Following your passion helps, but it still comes down to finding the motivation to keep going when times are tough and feelings of excitement are not as easy to hold onto.

8. Lack of capital- This common cause of failure happens mostly to new business owners. They did not have enough capital to start their business. They underestimated or wanted to cut corners on expenses. You have to have a reserve of capital to fall back on in an emergency to keep your doors open until business picks back up.

We talked about before that "broke" is the one problem you can't get around in a sale. It is something you can't survive for long as a business either. You have to find a way to generate capital to keep your business solvent. Money encourages money too in the same way that success encourages more success. Positivity brings opportunity. It is tougher to project positivity and success to potential clients or investors if you are stone broke and floundering. Having that seed money at the beginning and managing it wisely will go a long way to bringing your business success and a long way to staving off failure.

9 Lack of self-discipline- You have to be able to control yourself. This means attitude and how much you spend on items that you do not need among other things. If you want to master your business, you have to take care of and rid all the negative qualities about yourself. Don't be your own drag. Don't let your flaws doom you to downfall.

Following your passion can help you to stay on track, but it can also feed into some of the bad traits that cause you to lack self-discipline. People need to come into a vision with passion, but then run their business without being overrun or driven in decisions by emotion. That is a tough transition for most people. Running a business with emotion can cause you to be reactive and impulsive and even vengeful. None of these things are keys to success, and none of them help you to operate with self-discipline.

If you give another person power to control your emotions, you give them power to manipulate and destroy you. If you do not choose to control your own emotions with a commitment to self-discipline, you will destroy yourself. You will make bad choices, and you and everyone connected to you will pay for those bad, undisciplined choices.

10) **Lack of Ambition** – Ambition to rise above being average. Many of us get complacent or don't feel you should grow once you reach a certain level of success. You want to pay those that can help you achieve success. Buy the outfits that speak volumes, invest in your book, and develop a website and all the marketing tools you need to be seen and heard. You cannot get ahead in life if you are not willing to pay the price.

This goes back to the idea of risk, but it takes it a step further to look at what drives you to take those risks. When everything else is stripped away, do you have at your core a desire and a drive to be successful? Find that ambition for success.

Many things are out of our control in life, but many things are in our control. The above ten things can lead you to failure or can be adjusted in your life and your business in order to give you a better shot at success.

Secret Tip: Most people cannot see themselves as others see them.

Napoleon Hill wrote *Think and Grow Rich.* He emphasized many great ideas, including the 31 reasons people fail in business and in life. However, one great idea that he drove home was the ability to take a step back and see yourself the way others do. Some psychologists believe that the truest picture of who we are is what we think other people think of us. Do not mistake this to think I am telling you to care what other people think all the time. It does not mean you should live your life to please others. It just means that when we can begin to see ourselves the way that others might, we have a clearer picture of who we truly are and what that means for reaching our full potential and success.

Take time to ask your mom, dad, husband, wife, or close friend about how you are doing on these key traits of failure from this chapter. This will be more beneficial than you know. Teach yourself to build your brand. Study each trait by yourself as well. Once you have figured out if one or more of these traits are blocking your success, remove them and let's keep building. Take care of what you can control and all the rest will have much less power over you.

Chapter 8:
Have A Game Plan

"You must have a game plan.
If you aim at nothing, you'll hit it every time."

As a coach, I have spoken to people that have created success for themselves without having a business plan. Like many others, I failed to create business plans for some of the early businesses that I created. However, what I have found out through trial and error is that the person that starts with a business plan is far more likely to reach and attain their goals than a business owner that does not take the time to learn the market they are trying to influence and to plan accordingly.

✓ Business Plan & the Key Elements

SWOT- Let's get this broken down a little further in detail. In the previous chapter, we talked and touched on what a SWOT analysis is. It is a good tool for a reset as we said before. It is a very powerful tool for establishing your business plan from the beginning.

"Businesses often leave their greatest strength underutilized, and therefore they underperform their true potential in the market."

Strengths- Every business has strengths. You want to take this time to develop yours. What makes your business a strong brand and what makes you unique? You have to truly understand what makes you strong. If you don't take time to analyze this about yourself and your business, you are very likely to settle on secondary qualities that are not your strongest attribute or your best play. This is one way that we miss the mark when we fail to plan, and we don't run our SWOT analysis. Businesses often leave their greatest strength underutilized, and therefore they underperform their true potential in the market.

"The advantage of finding your own weaknesses is giving yourself the ability and the permission to address them yourself."

Weaknesses- Every business has something that the competition will hone in on to exploit. It's better if you take time to know for yourself where you could develop more. Weaknesses of a business can sometimes be personal, but we are mainly talking about what did you overlook before you opened your doors. Even if you are in business already, this is a perfect time to see why your business is or why your business is not taking off the way you intended.

The advantage of finding your own weaknesses is giving yourself the ability and the permission to address them yourself. You get to make corrections on your own terms. You get to make adjustments while you have choices about how to proceed. You have the chance to match your strengths and weaknesses in a way that you can plan your business to be the most prepared and the best equipped for success that you can be before you start or before you proceed any further.

"These are opportunities for you and for others."

Opportunities- When we look at your business, there are several reasons why you have chosen to open this particular business. What are you offering that no other business in your category is offering? Even if this means you are providing more jobs or the ability to open up a profession that students truly never get an opportunity to intern with and get on the job training for. These are opportunities for you and for others.

Opportunities are also your openings in the market. These are the places where others are neglecting or the blind spots others don't see. This is your chance to advance into new territory. It may play directly to your strengths, or it may be an opportunity for innovation where you are creating a new niche in the market just for yourself.

This is not the sort of thing you approach lightly or without planning. A completely new opportunity requires you to go in with your eyes open and a plan in place in order to have the best chance of success. Once others see you opening up a market, they will try to flood into that opportunity as well. You need to be prepared. Many will crash forward with no plan at all. They can cause problems for you, so you need to plan to handle that in order to claim success for yourself. Utilizing an opportunity you identify for your business means having a business plan in place.

"You would not go into battle without understanding the enemy, the terrain, and the threats that lie ahead."

Threats- Threats can take many forms. Sometimes they relate to your weaknesses. Some cannot be fully predicted, but that is no excuse to go into business without accessing all the threats you might face. You would not go into battle without understanding the enemy, the terrain, and the threats that lie ahead. You make a plan, so when things do surprise you, you are prepared to act instead of reacting with no plan at all.

This category in your business sometimes focuses on technology. Are you using outdated equipment that could not possibly serve your clients in a fast and efficient way? Say, for instance, when I was deciding to open a t-shirt company, I had to take into consideration all the companies like Vista Print and Custom Tees that had more technology and manpower than I had to be able to turn an order around in 24 hours or less. How could I get on this level of my competition? Did that mean I had to go out and buy equipment? I definitely was thinking that at first, and then I realize if you can't beat them, then join them. This was when I decided to outsource my printing to give my clients the same turnaround and great quality as well.

✓ Marketing Strategy

Sales- Often times we don't know if we have something that will sell on a massive level, so this is what makes this section so important in your business plan. I have been in sales all my life, and it never fails that with each new product or service you will launch in your business, you will have to figure out how to get it seen by your potential buyers.

Promotion - What platforms will you use to get your product seen? Video platforms such as Periscope, YouTube, Facebook or Instagram that promote imagery and short video clips or audio such as podcasting, radio, or possibly print, such as magazines. Each one of these platforms has their own culture and rules of engagement. Certain things reach and connect with these particular audiences while other behaviors turn them off. Some platforms may market well for your particular brand or desired audience while others may be off the mark for you. It can be overwhelming especially if all of this is outside your realm of experience or outside your comfort zone. There are so many ways to promote your business. It is only through trial and error that you will find what works best for you over the long term.

"Accidental and random marketing is no plan for success at all."

It does not hurt to seek help, and this may be where a success coach or a social media consultant as part of your marketing and strategy might be of help. You can consult with someone that knows these ropes and might be able to guide you to the best platforms for you and the best ways to utilize them. A marketing strategy and plan when it comes to whatever forms of free and paid media you use is vital. Accidental and random marketing is no plan for success at all.

Branding persona- Now that you have put all your elements of your business plan together, we have to figure out who you are and how you want to be represented in the public. Especially if the business you are promoting is you and your services, then you are part of the brand. In a very important way, you are marketing yourself. Investors and customers are very much buying into you as much or more than they are buying into your idea or product. This does not mean you open your private life up to every customer or individual trolling around the Internet. It does mean that you make conscious, planned decisions about what image you are projecting out to the world and your audience. You manage that image, and you use it to advance your business and what you are offering to the world. It matters how you are seen in the same way that the image and brand of your product and business matters.

Even if you are not branding your name, your business still needs a personal message that you want people to associate with you when they think of you. You will be surprised that many companies have been around for years and still don't know how to tell someone in 30 seconds or less who they are and what it is that they do. As an owner, you do not need a 30-page prospectus or an exhaustive history of your company for a customer to decide they want your product or service. They do need a connection. They need a clear idea of what you are and why that matters in a concise package.

They need an emotional response to your image and the thought of what you stand for. Your brand persona encapsulates that for the audience.

> *"Aiming at the entire world at once is aiming at nothing at all."*

Niche Market- How do you find your customers? This does not mean every customer or any customer. It means your customer. You have to target your ideal client in order to have a chance for real, sustained success. Aiming at the entire world at once is aiming at nothing at all. You need to understand your SWOT analysis, your marketing plan, and your brand well enough to pinpoint your ideal customer.

Your business plan in terms of identifying your ideal customer and your specific niche market should go so far as to be able to describe an individual. This can seem challenging, but the best way to find your target customers is to close your eyes and envision who will walk in your doors. This includes gender, height, and background, and past successes or failures of theirs. Let's take for example if you want to serve women and help them. You would ask yourself, why do I want to help these women, what type of problems would they be facing, and what's their background story that led them to my services, etc.?

So, perform this exercise for your business and your ideal customer. Is this ideal customer male or female? What is their age and education level? What is their background? What do they do and what is their family like? What region of the country and what type of neighborhood do they live in? What do they drive and where do they work? Once you identify all that, you can design your marketing to specifically connect with your niche market. You will better locate and persuade the customers best suited to your business then. The side effect is that by targeting your niche that specifically, you will still draw in customers outside that niche that connect with your business and brand too. You will not find or connect with anyone, if you cannot identify and target your niche to start with, though.

✓ Vision board

We use the vision board to see everything you have written down pictorially represented in front of you from your business plan to your goals both short term and long term. We want to see your personal aspirations and your professional dreams all laid out in a way that you can see and be reminded of daily.

"It keeps your 'why' in your face so that you don't forget."

Vision boards are not tools that all professionals think to employ. We've mentioned them a few times in previous chapters, but you may still not be convinced. This vision board is a collage. It shows where you want to go. Do you see yourself in the Bahamas on the beach celebrating your success or in the corner office overlooking the city? You can put up representations of both. You put up your business objectives too and a timeline for getting there. This is a time capsule of you looking forward from your business plan to the future. It is a visual reminder of what you are doing and why you are doing it to bring you back to your purposes and your desired outcomes. It keeps your "why" in your face so that you don't forget.

✓ Coaching/Mentor

A coach or mentor is someone to help you put it all together. Working as a business and success coach myself, I can tell you firsthand that there are a lot of pitfalls you can avoid by having a set of outside eyes on your business plan. You need someone you can trust and someone that is invested in your success. You can start with a sounding board of friends and colleagues. They can catch the things you overlook and play Devil's Advocate in a way you cannot do for yourself from the inside view. You don't want all positive and no constructive feedback, though. There comes a next phase where you need to also move to the mentor and coach then. You need to take on someone that can serve a deeper role of guidance for your business plan and its implementation. A good success coach can be those "outside eyes on the inside" for you. They can bring the skills and knowledge to the table that you may lack on your own to help you bring about the success you desire.

Often times we can get overwhelmed with starting, growing, and building our business. This step is essential, and if I had a coach like myself in my earlier days, I tell you I would not have wasted time, energy, or money the way I did through trial and error on my own. A coach can come in and tell you what they did wrong and right and where to get the most bang for your buck. You don't have to have a coach that runs a billion dollar corporation, but simply someone that you aspire to be like and that knows business from experience and study. This is exactly how I help all of my clients

I know you may say, I can't afford a coach right now, but I am here to tell you that yes, you can. In the next chapter, I will show you exactly how to find money where you least expect it.

Secret Tip: Don't be afraid to spend money on coaching.

Marketing that works is worth the investment. Coaching that works is worth ten times what you pay into it. Free advice is sometimes good, but sometimes it is worth every penny you paid for it and nothing more. We pay for the things we value. That investment, even a small investment, changes the game. It puts skin in the game for the coach and the person being coached to success. It matters. Do your due diligence and research who you are dealing with. Check references. Make a wise investment, but make an investment. Hiring on a success coach for the moment that you need them is a wise move that can help you more than you could know.

Contact me to talk through what success & business coaching means. I can walk you through what is involved and help you to make the right decision for you.

www.fitimamiller.com

Chapter 9:
Funding Your Ideas

"There is no five-step formula for making it in business"

In business, we often need to find a way to fund our idea, which means increasing our cash flow. While building your business, you may have thought of ways to help increase your income. We have also been told that multiple streams of income are needed to help sustain us until our business takes off. And if you believe that advice, you are thinking very wisely. There is no magic formula for launching a business. You need to build on your idea, and you need money to seed the growth of your business.

✓ Consider the nontraditional approaches.

The first thing most people think of is traditional approaches to financing. We look at business loans, loans from family or friends, or other outside investors. Many of these traditional approaches require a show of income and viability. Even family is tough to approach for serious investment before you have results to show. Banks want collateral and assets. The truth is that investment might be in the future of your business in later phases, but it is not the first step. Angel investors are a next step growth process. Let's look at how you begin from the bottom and get creative with diversifying your sources of income to get started.

I funded my business the non-traditional way through a refund check that I received from my MBA program. I will never forget when I got that $3,500 check in the mail. Honestly, that was my only source of income at the time since I decided to stay home and take care of my ill sister. I was able to use only $3,500 to grow and build my brand. In just one year, it was valued at $30,000.00. After looking back, it doesn't seem like much compared to some business empires, but I can guarantee you that no one else in my program was thinking to use that refund check as a business loan.

There are so many ways we can find additional income, especially when we think about creating a secondary or third income. You may even think at this point you have to bring in $10,000 from this and $5,000 from that to make any of this work. If you can pull this off, that's incredible, but for most that is generally not the case.

"You see I wasn't making six figures between all of this, but it was all positive cash flow, and that's what you want."

I decided to write resumes for family and friends for a nominal fee, work a job as a project manager, coach on the side and took on an artist and two models to manage. By adding all of these additional sources of income, it would help me to continue to fund my business while helping others in the process. You see I wasn't making six figures between all of this, but it was all positive cash flow, and that's what you want.

"Consistent success is needed in order to justify letting up on lines of support for your business."

The future of these endeavors is dependent upon your goals. If you are satisfied with $1500 per month, then that determines how long you keep these sources of income open. If it is $5000, then you need to keep working on your income and maintain side jobs longer. You should have a business that sustains you for a year or more at your level of comfort before you look at cutting off sources of financing in order to focus on other aspects of the business. That consistent success is needed in order to justify letting up on lines of support for your business.

✓ Diversification allows more opportunity for wealth creation.

Diversification simply means having the ability to find a means to create wealth or money from different avenues. The more lines of support you have for your business, the greater your growth potential will be. Diversification creates stability during the difficult beginnings of a business. Consider multiple sources of cash flow in order to make this possible even if your resources may seem limited.

Have you ever thought of investing in stocks? I'm sure the thought has crossed your mind, but for some reason, it seemed too complex, or you didn't know who to trust. I will be the first to admit it was the furthest thing from my mind until my husband came home with a suggestion to invest in penny stock with fidelity to learn the market. After we had talked, he felt comfortable enough to make a larger investment into Angie's list. After talking with him, we both subscribed to Motley Fool, a subscription site for serious investors to learn the trends of the ForEX trade market. I became intrigued about investing. I was researching day and night and bought a host of books at Barnes and Noble on investing. After understanding the market, we decided it would be wise to invest in his company stock that would allow him to buy at 15% lower than market value as an employee discount. Instantaneously, he was able to give himself a raise just by investing in company stock. Starting with $150.00, six months later he made $1,000. That was almost a 300% profit margin. I wanted to share this story with you because he actually took that $1,000 and invested in into his master's program. Once he made an "A," the company would reimburse him, and he would take that $1,000 and invest on the second opportunity, the third, and so on and so forth. You see, by him investing $150.00 in that stock, he didn't realize that small investment would pay for his entire master's with no further cash out of pocket and no student loans with high interest.

"In business, we have to take risks and those risks may seem harsh and life-changing at the time, but it's necessary to achieve the goals that you desire."

That's absolutely mind-blowing to most. It's all about putting your money or time in different places that will seemingly work out for your best interest. All that income can build upon itself as seen in the chart below.

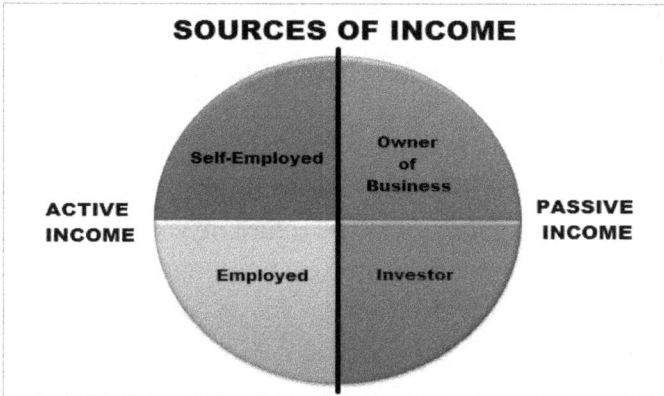

Exhibit C: Multiple Streams of Income

5 streams of income and how it worked for me

- Work- took a job as a project manager
- Stock Market- Bought penny stocks
- (401k)- My husband could pull from if needed
- Schooling- refund check
- Hobby- Artist management and model management
- Savings- Did not have any at the time

You may not have all of these sources of income, but there are almost definitely three for sure you could use to your advantage. In business we have to take risks and those risks may seem harsh and life-changing at the time, but it's necessary to achieve the goals that you desire. This is how I stayed afloat while in the growing phase of my business. It's all about how to find non-traditional and traditional ways to start to grow and build your business.

✓ Cutting luxuries can give you breathing room.

When times get tough, we also have to think about how we spend our money and the ways we can save money – just until we have a positive return in our business. You always have to know rainy days will come and if that isn't the truth, then I don't know what the truth is. Not thinking about the future of your business may be the greatest mistake you can make. Trust me, in business, rainy days will come and you want to be as prepared as possible. Diversification helps as we discussed above, but cutting costs, and luxuries, in particular, allow those sources of income to stretch much further.

If you want to find money, I will tell you first hand that cutting out on all the luxuries gives ourselves breathing room. It's only for a short period of time, but I know you can do it. You don't have to get your nails and hair done every two weeks. That will save approximately $2,000 a year. Don't buy the newest iPhone or new car trying to "keep up with the Joneses." You can save so much if you take a moment or two to learn to do it yourself instead of paying someone else to do it. Avoid buying high price items in the department store. Do you really need that Michael Kor's plain t-shirt for $24.99 or will a $7.99 one do just fine?

Now that you are saving redirect that money into places that will gain value. That will include stocks, bonds, mutual funds, schooling, or trade training. Use these channels of income to funnel into your business.

Secret Tip: Don't be afraid to invest in your business now and save later. This may seem like unusual advice compared to what many financial experts tell you. It is the reality of entrepreneurship, though. There is a certain amount of risk that you have to take to strike out on your own. Part of that risk is putting your money back into your business and putting off the savings that others might count on. That does not mean you will never have savings. It does mean that for a few years of building up your business all your money is committed. Once you reach your success goals, then more traditional savings practices will begin. Don't feel bad about this. Take a gamble on yourself.

Chapter 10:
Never Reveal Your Plan

"Sharing is caring, but not in business."

This story is very personal to me and will be an excellent example of how I can use my mistakes to help you avoid pitfalls on your road to success. This is where a success coach could have guided me out of troubled waters. This book and good coaching can help you too in this way. So, take heed of the story, the warning, and the lesson this chapter contains.

> *"The world is full of unscrupulous people that are looking for ways to steal ideas from you instead of coming up with any of their own."*

I gave up a million dollar idea by not realizing I was engaging with a predatory scammer with my business idea. The world is full of unscrupulous people that are looking for ways to steal ideas from you instead of coming up with any of their own. They will take what is yours, especially your intellectual property, and try to make a quick buck any way they can. Let's take the steps now to educate ourselves about this so that you can save yourself a great deal of trouble down the line.

✓ My Idea ...

I have always been an innovator with a creative mind able to think of ideas that would create an insurmountable amount of wealth if I could just get them seen or backed financially. In 2008, I had an idea that was sure to solve the problem many mothers had faced with newborns. My idea was a method for carrying and then mixing baby formula with water at the time it was needed. I had a name for it, I knew why it was a product people needed and would want, and I was ready to see if I could get it out into the market. I did not know the way to do so, and that is where I ran into trouble by trusting the wrong people.

✓ Where Things Went Wrong ...

I reached out to an invention company that I saw advertise their services on a late night program channel. After speaking with the representative, I received a package in the mail to fill out and submit my idea along with a drawing that would eventually become my 4d prototype. After looking back and knowing what I know about most invention companies, I would have saved my idea until I could create, package, and promote it myself.

"What I know now has helped me to help others avoid the same mistakes."

At this point, they wanted $10,000 I did not have. This was the cost just for a digital prototype. They wanted this amount to draw my idea on a computer. I should have known there was a problem, but I was young and did not have the experience I have now. With every setback, there is an equal gain in learning and experience.

What I know now has helped me to help others avoid the same mistakes.

They agreed to keep my information on file for twelve months. Later, they would contact me again to ask for any other ideas. I would again miss this red flag and told them another idea I had for a multi-color nail polish in one container.

✓ Discovering the Problem ...

Around 2009 or 2010, my husband and I were in TJ Max and spotted a product on the shelves that looked exactly like the bottle idea I had first given to this invention company. I suspected my idea might have been stolen as there had been no product like it before. Often first run product ideas are released in stores like T J Max before they go wide to a mainstream audience. Despite my suspicions, I would go on and end up giving this company my second idea. I still thought at the time that the development of this product I discovered was possibly a coincidence.

It was a year or two later that I would see my nail polish idea show up in a Dollar General by a well known cosmetic line that is normally carried in their stores. This was when I knew I had been cheated and my ideas along with all the money the invention company could have made me were lost.

✓ From Setbacks to Equivalent Greatness ...

The FTC (Federal Trade Commission) has cracked down on this company and found that they have stolen and sold hundreds of ideas of potential clients. There are endless stories like mine, and a lawsuit was filed to help with damages of inventors. I am still working toward regaining compensation for what was taken from me. You have to remember in business before you share your idea you have to have done your homework with the individuals you are engaging with. Trust is never something you should take lightly when going into business. Trusting that this company had my best interests was a huge mistake, but with every negative experience, a positive lesson was learned. I learned that I had the ability to become a millionaire again in my own right.

"Always do your due diligence."

I'm not going to call this company out by name in the venue of this book. Just know that there are many companies just like the one that cheated me. Always do your due diligence by searching for scam alerts or customer/employee reviews. In business, the Internet is your best friend in this regard. I learned to protect my work, my art, and my names that will be introduced in the world, which is ultimately my brand.

✓ Do It Yourself Success ...

You can do your own research and save yourself a lot of money and trouble by applying for your own trademarks, patents, and copyrights. It does take some work and study, but every new thing you learn and each new skill you pick up along this process is another potential source of income and advancement for you. It represents another path of diversification for you as you are starting your business even as you are saving yourself money. In my case, I was able to provide these services to others for much less than it would cost them to seek it out from patent attorneys or others that do this same work.

It often costs as much as $3000 for the preparation of an application to the trademark office from a trademark attorney. Even after submitting the application, there is no guarantee that your application will be accepted even if prepared properly. It can be as long as an 18-month process. I was able to do this myself for a fraction of the cost at only $500. I also submitted in multiple categories and got my first trademark from my own preparation without having to rely on others to do it for me. My first registered trademark was WHEW, the program that I offer to women to help build them from a personal and professional standpoint. WHEW is growing to be the first success institute of learning for women all over the world.

If you don't have the cash on hand to fully register your name or logo you can also put the "TM" trademark symbol beside your product name. That act only protects your idea and name in that particular state. The registered trademark protects you nationwide. Putting a "C" copyright symbol in the proper place on your work protects it for eighteen months. Other forms of copyright filing come with other protections and timelines. You can work with copyright in a similar way. Under the current law, your written work is under copyright the moment you create it. With computers and electronic tracking, this is much easier to prove and provide a trail through e-mail and other means to defend your copyright. Still, you can rely on the tried and true method of the "poor man's copyright" or the "dead man's copyright" as it is called. This is the act of mailing a hard copy of work or designs to yourself through the mail. The envelope remains sealed and kept in a safe place until such time that you need to prove your copyright. That sealed envelope establishes proof of the time period of creation and ownership. If you are smart about this, you can send a zip file of all the logos, artwork, or words you want copyright and pay one fee. Whatever is inside that zip file is protected. Most companies will not reveal this type of information, due to you cutting in on the profit they can make by charging you a $49 or $99 fee for each item submitted.

It is important to note the proper ways and times to trademark and copyright. If you put a copyright mark in the wrong place on an intellectual property, you might have issues. Director George A. Romero put a copyright next to the original title of his first movie instead of below on the script in the proper place. At the time, it issued copyright over the title instead of the material itself. As a result, when the title was changed, he lost the copyright on his first film, and the movie became public domain from that point forward. Do your due diligence to avoid losing your ideas and property.

> *"In these cases, the money should not matter as much as the value of locking down your brand idea."*

A patent is more expensive than a trademark. There are times when that is worth it, though. Products we discussed earlier in the book like the Snuggie or Pillow Pets exploded onto the market and created a financial empire. Having those products patented was well worth the cost for their inventors. When you are ready to start your brand, this is something to consider. In these cases, the money should not matter as much as the value of locking down your brand idea. You don't ever really know what will take off and what won't, but if you believe in something enough to start your business, you should believe in it enough to protect it. You need to put in that research, work and cost to see that your idea remains yours.

https://www.uspto.gov/trademark

or

https://www.uspto.gov/

The above links go to the United States Trademark Office. You can find the application form there and then do the research to understand how to properly complete the application. You can hire a success coach like myself who has the experience to walk you through it cheaper and more effectively than other services out there. You can and should do your due diligence to seek out professional help from proper and reputable attorneys in your local area in the field too as needed.

With the Internet and other resources out there, there is no excuse for not finding out all you can about these subjects before you begin. Part of that diligence needs to be in exhaustive product research to be certain that the idea you came up with is not already patented and in production. You do not want to waste time and money applying for a patent to a similar product that is already patented. Do what is required to protect your work and business.

✓ Your Dreams Are Worth It ...

After sharing my story, I hope that this encourages you to go after your dreams and achieve anything that your mind can conceive. When it's all said and done, it's all about protecting your work and putting in the work to see your success become a reality.

Secret tip: Don't be afraid to put in work and do your own research.

By reviewing and studying all the videos on the USPTO, I was able to learn how to flawlessly submit my own trademark application and inventor's paperwork. That saved me thousands of dollars and attorney fees. Now I am an expert on trademarks and will be able to do this for anyone that needs my help. I added an extra stream of income to my business by helping others learn to do it themselves too.

It may seem draining and exhausting, but it is worth it. You'll find you are capable of far more than you ever realized. It is imperative that you take the lead on protecting your ideas and work. This is all the work and preparation needed for your future success. The hours of research were worth it for me. They were worth it for the brand and idea I was creating, and that work has continued to pay off for me with subsequent business ventures. Knowledge is power, and that power will lead to your success.

About the Author

Fitima Miller is an entrepreneur, empowerment speaker, author, designer, business growth strategist, super coach and mindset guru. Fitima is dedicated to providing coaches, small business owners, and entrepreneurs with the tools they need to create a meaningful career while living their best lives. She should not have made it this far. With all the challenges in her youth stacked against her, she rose above the odds to surprise everyone with her success. Fitima represents fearlessness and courage even in her darkest hour. The impossible became the possible with faith, hard work, and dedication.

Fitima is no stranger to the world of startups. She began her life of entrepreneurship at the tender age of 14. Through her persistent can do attitude Fitima set out to make a difference in the world. She graduated from Shaw University with a Bachelors in Business Administration and Management reaching this goal within 2 ½ years and all the while on the Dean's List. She also completed her Master's Degree in Business Administration and Leadership from Laurel University where she maintained her position on the Dean's List as well.

Fitima has helped develop workshops and programs that have transformed the lives of men and women. Fitima Miller represents a woman of excellence. She is an advocate for those who lack the tenacity and knows how to run a thriving business, and she provides her clients with the resources and knowledge to be successful. She is the founder of the Native Chick Clothing brand, a t-shirt line that empowers and inspires women of the world to stand up for what they believe in through a host of slogans that support maintaining healthy relationships. Leading by example, she started a nonprofit called Dream of Peace to assist at-risk youth with life skills. During this time, she saw a real need not only to encourage and promote self-sufficiency she took it one step further and became a foster parent to teen girls ranging in age from 12-18. Developing these leadership skills led her to continue to empower young ladies through G.E.LG., a girl empowerment leadership group that reassures girls to embrace their aspirations in life, achieving them by building self-confidence and awareness of self.

Want to know more?

To contact Fitima Miller for speaking engagements, seminars, workshops, training or business coaching opportunities ...

Visit

www.fitimamiller.com

She is also the founder of **Time is Money Tour,** a **Business Speed Coaching** program that she created to dissect anyone's business in 30 minutes or less and provide feedback on the next steps they should take in order to achieve their goals.

She is also the creator and a founder of **WHEW**, a program designed to help women in business or looking to go into business through professionally developed content offered online.

More details and information on all of these programs and how you can get involved and utilize these services can be found at **www.fitimamiller.com.**

Acknowledgments

The success of this project has been dependent on the wisdom and support I received from many people on a personal and professional level. The reason for writing this book came from the many questions I received from clients as a coach, from family, from friends that had business questions, and even strangers that walked up to me asking for business advice. I am so grateful for all my coaches and mentors that took the time to help me understand that my truth, struggles, wisdom and knowledge would help other entrepreneurs transform their dream into reality.

Special thanks to my father Ronald Harris Sr. who showed me as a little girl what it meant to be great, to never give up, and to always finish the race no matter what stands in your way as it relates to business and life. To my mother Sylvia Rochelle, you taught me what it means to help and give to others without asking anything in return.

Through her endless generosity, my sister Kawanda was the definition of support and was able to make this book possible for me. To my brother Renoldo, I thank you for listening to all my millions of ideas and providing feedback that was truly needed at crunch time. Big thanks to my brother Ryan Harris, you are the sweetest and smartest kid I know. Thank you for always believing in your sister. I am so thankful to have my brother Ronald Jr in my life. Thank you for listening to your sister's business ideas, while you were studying in med school, giving me advice, and making me feel that I could accomplish anything.

I am especially grateful for my stepmother Miranda Harris. Words can't express how lucky I am to have a mother who has her daughter's back at all times. I thank you for the childcare and the ongoing love and support you provide for my family and me. Grandma Gloria Dale, what would I do without you, my spiritual healer? I love you past the galaxy. Thank you for knowing my heart.

I am grateful for dedicated and supportive friends. All of you have played a major role in my life and watched me grow into the person I am today. I thank you for all the phone calls, love, support, and showing up to my events, providing honest feedback. You guys are definitely my rocks -- Chan Hall, Mya Cullins, Kamilah Wirtz, Marshall Scott.

Jack Deuterman, you have been a great business coach, in terms of helping me with my numbers for my business and brainstorming new ideas. I would also like to thank my branding coach Ken Canion. Even though we just recently met, you have been a tremendous help to my business. Your passion and generosity to share your expert comments, feedback on my book and the direction of my business have been unbelievable.

And most importantly, there are few words that adequately describe my appreciation for my husband Warren Keith Miller Jr., who has spent endless hours listening, brainstorming, and supporting any project I do from day one. I thank you for sharing the care for our children to help me reach and attain my goals. You are everything a wife could ask for in a husband.

List Your Top 10 Reasons Why "You" will never give up on your dreams.

1.

2.

3.

4.

5.

6.

7.

8.

9.

10.

"SUCCESS AND NOTHING LESS"
-Fitima Miller-

www.ingramcontent.com/pod-product-compliance
Lightning Source LLC
Chambersburg PA
CBHW071447200326
41519CB00019B/5650